O9-BTJ-647

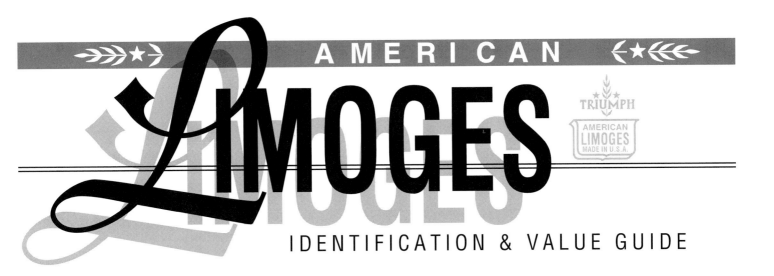

AMERICAN LIMOGES

IDENTIFICATION & VALUE GUIDE

Raymonde Limoges

COLLECTOR BOOKS

A Division of Schroeder Publishing Co., Inc.

The current values in this book should be used only as a guide. They are not intended to set prices, which vary from one section of the country to another. Auction prices as well as dealer prices vary greatly and are affected by condition as well as demand. Neither the Author nor the Publisher assumes responsibility for any losses that might be incurred as a result of consulting this guide.

Searching For A Publisher?

We are always looking for knowledgeable people considered to be experts within their fields. If you feel that there is a real need for a book on your collectible subject and have a large comprehensive collection, contact us.

Cover Design: Beth Summers
Book Design: Benjamin R. Faust

Additional copies of this book may be ordered from:

COLLECTOR BOOKS
P.O. Box 3009
Paducah, KY 42002-3009

– or –

RAYMONDE LIMOGES
P.O. Box 73263
Puyallup, WA 98373-0263

@ $24.95. Add $2.00 for postage and handling.

Copyright: Raymonde Limoges, 1996

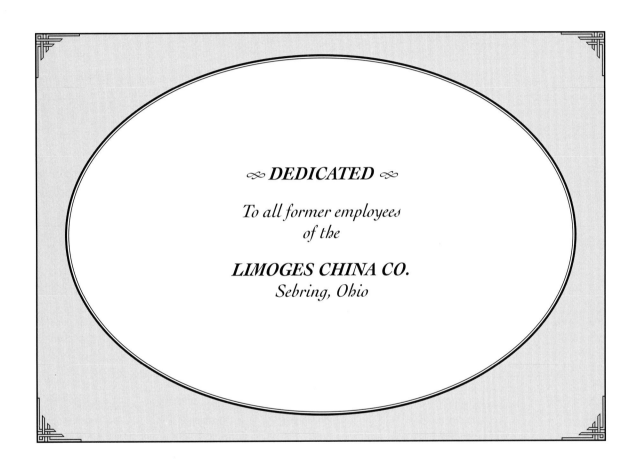

∽ *DEDICATED* ∽

To all former employees
of the

LIMOGES CHINA CO.
Sebring, Ohio

ACKNOWLEDGMENTS

Thank You

A book is the result of many hands and many hours.

My appreciation to all who helped in making this become a reality, for the bits of information gleaned from the many pages; for ideas, comments, suggestions, shopping trips, late hours of typing, early telephone calls, correspondence; for your patience, moral support, and friendship, I am grateful.

American Legion Post 166, Alliance, OH
Anderson, Terry
Baker, Howard
Ball, Francis
Banks, Ed
Barelaud, Mme. Colette
Barni, Annie & Christian
Barrett, Frank
Bowen, Barbara
Calhoon, Nancy
Cameron, Mary Ann
Cannell, Daphne & John
Carnaby Antique Mall, Puyallup, WA
Collectors News, Grundy Center, IA
Columbiana Antique Gallery, OH
De Muth, Henry
Deskins, Sheryl
Driscoll, Donna
Ellenburg, Wilma
Engelburg Antiks
Fahnert, Alice & John
Farberware, Inc., NY
Freighthouse Antiques
Good Housekeeping Inc., NY
Gorin-Kellner, Ann
Greenamayer Country Store Antiques
Griffith, Ellie & Ed
H & H Antiques
Harley, Debbie
Hjeltness, Diane J.
Howells, Jocelyn
Ivory Manor
Juszczak, Donna
Keller, Harrison
Limoges, Gloria
Limoges, Marthe & Real
Mac's Barn
Mary
Memory Lane Antiques
Meunier, Armande

Muldoon, Linda
Museum of Ceramics, Youngstown, OH
Naders, Linda & Al
Ohio Historical Society
Old Stuff Antique Newspaper
Parks, JoAnn & Bob
Pate, Nancy
Peddler's Stop Antiques
Peterson, Gerald
Pierce County Library, Tacoma, WA
Poutre, Therese & Raymond
Puyallup Public Library, Puyallup, WA
Ripple, Glen
Rodman Public Library, Alliance, OH
Rudolph, Katherine
Russell, Mona
L & D Jensen
Schreckengost, Viktor
Sebring High School Library, Sebring, OH
Sebring Historical Society, Sebring, OH
Sebring Public Library, Sebring, OH
Slabaugh, Marilyn
Smith, Betty
Smith, Carlos
Stagecoach Antiques
Steed, J & Jan
Stoffer, Betty
Strasburg Antiques
Sullivan, Helen
Surls, Harry
Tacoma Public Library, Tacoma, WA
The Shop, Kent, WA
Thornsley, Paul
UW Engineering Library, Patent Dept.
Union Station Antiques, Greentown, OH
University of Toledo, OH
Verner, Tom
Watkins, Virginia
Wuchnic, Sandra
Yaggi, Eleanor

CONTENTS

INTRODUCTION

As a longtime collector and dealer of fine china, my special interest is Limoges, old and new, the white porcelain made in my native country of France.

Saturday markets are great places to look for treasures. On such a trek, my husband George, also an avid collector, found a plate with a familiar design. The decor was a very popular decal by Fragonard, similar to our Limoges set. The 50¢ price tag was a bargain. The backstamp was new to us: Love Seat by American Limoges. It was in 1982 and the first step of a long journey. Thousands of miles and as many stops later, at flea markets, antique shops, and garage sales, the collection grew to become a passion. Hours spent at the library looking for material on American Limoges guided our path to Sebring, Ohio.

Several people answered our newspaper ad in regard to the Limoges plant. In June 1990, we arrived, like tourists, cameras and tape recorder in hand, for an interview with Mr. Harrison Keller, former head of the Limoges China Co. It was a delightful dinner. The idea of a book was welcomed by Mr. Keller who said, "It would be proper, logical, and I would support it." On that trip, we also met Daphne, the president of the newly formed Sebring Historical Society, and her husband Jack. Looking for Limoges through tons of dishes stacked in a warehouse was like Christmas shopping. On the same occasion, we met Virginia, who was to become a close friend and an expert on Limoges dishes, as well as many former employees.

Collecting has taken us through highways and byways, traveling to see America, meeting strangers who became friends.

Today, almost 15 years since Love Seat came to our house, the collection has increased to more than 2,000 pieces.

In 1689, a family ancestor, Pierre Amant, Sieur de Jolycoeur de Limoges, came to New France, now the Province of Quebec, in the name of King Louis XIV of France. The name was shortened to Pierre Limoges, in 1716. Pierre and his wife, Catherine, had 8 children. There are many descendants living in the U.S. and in Canada.

THE AMERICAN LIMOGES CHINA CO.

Limoges is the name of a city in France, where porcelain has been manufactured for more than 200 years. Hundreds of names have become associated with the trade, since the Massie Brothers & Grelet produced the first wares in 1771. One of the largest and best known companies, Haviland China, was started in 1842 and shipped huge amounts of dinnerware. Limoges porcelain is lightweight, pure white, and translucent, sometimes bearing different backstamps. The green stamp is the name of the manufacturer and others are names of decorators or importers.

American Limoges was made in Ohio, from 1897 to 1957 by the Sebring brothers. The chinaware is soft paste, creamy white, and heavy. Most pieces are crazed and have only one backstamp.

What became the American Limoges China Co. was started in 1900 by Frank Sebring, the factory was named Sterling China. It was to make the finest thin tableware in America, comparable to the European imports. Clays, chemicals, and knowledge were imported to start the production. It was marked Sterling China and should be of fine porcelain. A pottery in East Liverpool was also called Sterling.

The name was changed to Sebring China, but the Sebring Pottery had moved from East Liverpool. It became so confusing that the mail arriving at the post office was opened by a clerk from each company to decide where it should go. (McKee). "Little salable ware was produced and not being one to complacently watch the open bung-hole F A quickly converted to the manufacturing of the wares he knew how to make," (McKee, *The Second Oldest Profession*). So it is doubtful that much, if any, of the wares marked Sterling China are still around. The trademarks used during that time period are uncertain. (See the backstamp section, number 2A & 2.)

In 1903, the factory was partially destroyed by a fire. Fred was the new owner/manager when it reopened, but the production of fine china ended. In 1904, it became Limoges China Co., until the 1940s when "American" was added to the name. It was the first plant to have a tunnel kiln rather than the beehive, a full time artist to make original design not copies of English-style decor, a permanent ceramic laboratory, and a machine to apply decals.

In 1915, the Jewel Tea Co. awarded a contract to the Limoges China Co. for 52 carloads of 30-pc. sets, to be made within a year and delivered in cartons rather than barrels.

In 1920, 45,000 pieces were manufactured daily.

On September 26, 1924, at the celebration of the town's 25th anniversary, a 42-pc. set of dinnerware by Limoges was given to the oldest person attending. Neither the name of the recipient nor if there was a special marking on that set of dishes is known. In 1946, a service was made "exclusively for Mr. Pollock, in appreciation of his 20 years of service to the School System by the Board of Education of Sebring, Ohio."

Limoges made dinnerware, souvenirs, calendar plates, tea sets, and children's dishes. In the early years, many companies used the same decals imported from Germany. Identification is not positive unless the blanks can be matched with a marked piece. In the 1930s, the company experimented with colored glaze, such as Golden Glow, Emerald Glow, Ivory Ware, and a pale pink called Peach Blow.

A dozen or so pottery manufacturers joined forces to become the American Chinaware Corporation with offices in the Central Tower Building in Cleveland. The business venture's collapse in 1931 left many in financial ruin. The Sebrings, not a part of the corporation, consolidated their plants. The Limoges plant was the only one to continue production during the Depression. To stimulate sales, merchandising included door to door sales, installment plans, theater give-aways, or furniture store specials. Drugstores and grocery stores used punch cards or coupons and a piece of china would be free for a certain amount spent at the store. Newspapers would offer coupons for subscriptions to be exchanged at redemption centers. Soaps and cereals boxes would contain pieces of dinnerware, a selection offered with different size boxes. Sales were made also through large retailers and department stores.

In 1934, a young artist, Viktor Schreckengost, born in Sebring and a graduate of the Cleveland Art Institute, introduced some popular lines of dinnerware. A well-known designer at the time, he was working for the Limoges, the Salem, and the Sebring plants. Triumph, Victory, Diana, and Jiffy Ware are some of his creations.

The big event for the pottery trade was the annual Pittsburgh Show, held in January at the William Penn Hotel. At the show, new products were introduced and the buyers decided what would be fashionable for the dinner table. The quality and prices of American Limoges dinnerware was comparable to others made in the region at the time.

Starting in 1931, and again after WWII, the Syndicat des Porcelainiers (32 companies, including Haviland) and the City of Limoges (France) Chamber of Commerce filed a lawsuit through the U.S. State Department. The Sebrings had used the name "Limoges" before the turn of the century when in East Palestine, Ohio. Their plant, the Ohio China Co., advertised as a "manufacturer of Limoges porcelain, plain and decorated, with the backstamp as logo." See the first mark in the backstamp section.

The name Limoges is a "restricted name," protected by law to be used for the porcelain manufactured in or around the city of Limoges, France, and with clays from the region. Since the name was often associated with the Havilands, it was only fair to protect and inform the consumer as to what they were buying. Because of that resolution, the name was changed to include American. In the 1940 Sebring High School yearbook, page 108, the sponsor is listed as "American Limoges China Inc." A shield, designed in part by Harrison Keller, was used as the new company logo. Mr. Keller was with the company from 1937 until June 1948 when he became head of the Salem China Pottery.

Harry Bloomberg, a salesman from Boston, became the new owner of the Limoges and the Warwick China in Wheeling, WV. In 1955, members of the alumni of NYU attempted the purchase of both plants. The transaction was unsuccessful and they were returned to Bloomberg.

Production was stopped in 1955. Like many other potteries struggling against the new plastics, inexpensive imports, the dishwasher, and the high cost of labor, the Limoges China Co. could not compete on the market. Manager F.W. Pipolo continued negotiations, searching for financial help, and even using the employees' vacation fund. Bloomberg filed for Chapter 11 on March 10, 1956. In July 1956, work was started again with a one year credit extension. James Talcott Inc., a N.Y. finance company, started foreclosure proceedings in 1957.

The Limoges China Co. ended on April 9, 1958, when it was sold for $63,500, at a Mahoning county sheriff's sale.

Today, some parts of the plant are still standing quietly among the weeds. Trains pass through the village without a second look at the once busy loading docks.

If old bricks could talk...

SEBRING, OHIO

Sebring, Ohio, was born in 1899, the dream child of the Sebring family. The small town became one of the centers of the pottery industry.

The Sebrings, who were experienced potters for several generations, came to East Liverpool in 1864. The area along the Ohio river was, at the time, the largest pottery district in the country. In 1887, the five brothers bought the old Agner-Gaston Pottery in East Liverpool and changed its name to Sebring Brothers Pottery. In 1898, they owned a 5-kiln factory called the "Klondyke."

In 1893, Fred, with other partners, managed the Ohio China Co. in East Palestine where Limoges China was already being made. They were successful and had great dreams to have a pottery town of their own.

Searching for the perfect location of their new town, they settled along the Mahoning River a few miles away. With 2,000 acres of farmland serviced by the railroad, the purchase involved about a dozen farm families, with the largest portions being the Stephen Gray, the Allison, and the William Johnson farms. The Gray farmhouse was used as a starting point for the development of the new community. Plans were drawn, secretly at first, and the official proclamation was made on May 8, 1898.

The new settlement was to be a model city. The streets were numbered and the avenues bore the names of the States of the Union. The building sites were allocated by lottery and a clause in the deeds prohibited the sale of intoxicating beverages, except to the drugstore for medicinal purposes only. Building of the potteries was started at once along the railroad.

The first pottery was the Oliver China Pottery. It opened in 1899 with 250 employees, Oliver Sebring as manager. Then the Sebring Pottery opened with Frank Sebring in charge. The French and the Sterling China (Limoges) Potteries were soon in operation. The Saxon Pottery opened in May of 1911. The Sebring brothers were buying, selling, and managing each other's companies.

With paved streets, utilities, a post office, two banks, and a land company, more businesses became part of this fine village. The Pennsylvania Railroad made a station with a parked box car in November 1899. A doctor, dentist, and a jeweler moved in the business section. Mr. Albright was the first mayor.

The first newspaper, *The Sebring News* was published June 8, 1899. The residential district of nice homes was developed as more employees came to live in town. The Sebrings built expansive and fashionable homes situated on corner lots. The price of the average home was between $1,000 and $5,000. The George Sebring residence is estimated to have cost $12,000, according to a bid in June 1898.

Churches and fraternal and charitable organizations were started. The first Methodist church was finished just in time for the wedding of Miss Pearl Sebring, Oliver's daughter, to Mr. Homer Taylor of Knowles, Taylor & Knowles, in December 1901.

A one-room schoolhouse was opened in 1900. Among other "firsts" were a bowling alley, three pool tables, and a Grand Opera Company. The town had its very own football, baseball, and basketball teams.

The industries prospered. At one time the potteries' work force was 1,200 strong, boasting 25 ware kilns, 24 decorating kilns, on 226,000 sq. ft. of floor space.

The trains ran continuously through town, first bringing the building materials necessary to build the new town, coal and oil to fire the kilns, clay from Kentucky and West Virginia to make the china, and finally shipping the finished wares.

An automobile industry started in 1912 was short lived. It built a car called the Sebring Six. Racing at the Indianapolis Speedway was another expensive model called the Big Six.

The town survived the big snow of 1910 and the floods of 1924. It weathered the depression years, the strikes, unemployment, and the fires. Fire was a constant danger. In 1920, a complete block including *The Sebring Times* and the town's early papers went in smoke. In July 1931, another blaze in the local auto dealership burned the garage and 42 cars. The Oliver Sebring residence was destroyed on Thanksgiving, 1943. In 1947, the Grindley Art Manufacturing Co. burned to the ground. The Royal China Co., started in June 1934 in the old E. H. Sebring plant, burned in 1970.

The factories closed, the people moved away.

Today, it is a quiet town with beautiful trees shading the mostly residential neighborhoods.

In 1920, Sebring had 3,540 habitants. In 1990, 4,848 habitants called it home.

THE SEBRING FAMILY

Born to a family of modest potters and working in the local plants, the children of George and Elizabeth were industrious and ambitious. Starting their own town and becoming successful businessmen, from the Gray farmhouse to the large factories they managed, earned them the name "Sensational Sebrings."

All have called Grandview Cemetery, in Sebring, their final resting place.

William Henry (1870 – 1904)

He was involved in the pottery business with his brother Frank. William was killed at the railroad crossing on Black Friday, Dec. 9, 1904. At the time, he was foreman of the decorating department of the Limoges China Co. With his wife, Eva Huston Sebring, he had two children, Earl E. and Virginia.

Frederick E. (1868 – 1925)

Born in East Liverpool, October 4, 1868, Fred, as he was known, founded the pottery that was to become the Limoges China Co. In 1911 he erected the Saxon China Co., sold it in 1917, and went into real estate. A heart attack ended his life on Dec. 13, 1925, on returning from a stay in Sebring, FL. Fred was a charter member of several social and fraternal organizations in Sebring. With his wife, Katherine Surls, he had two daughters.

Joseph (1862 – 1890)

He died at age 28 of pneumonia.

Oliver Howard (1857 – 1929)

Oliver was born July 14, 1857, in East Liverpool. The first pottery built in Sebring was named after O.H. because he was the oldest of the brothers. He was president of the French China Co. The Sebring Manufacturing Corporation in 1925, combining the French, the Saxon China, and the Strong Manufacturing Co. He was also president of the Citizen's Banking Co. Director, and Vice-president of the Knowles, Taylor, and Knowles Pottery, and was involved in other business ventures. In 1878, he married Mathilda Hume and had four daughters and a son, Bert H. Sebring. He died July 27, 1929.

Frank Albert (1865 – 1936)

Born in Vanport, PA, July 20, 1865, Frank married in Sept. 1884, to M.L. Harbison and had six children. At the time of his death, he was president of the Limoges China Co. and chairman of the board of directors of the Sebring Pottery Co. and the Salem China Co.

Ellsworth Henry (1861 – 1937)

In 1931 he retired from the pottery business and enjoyed citrus farming in Florida where he died in 1937. E.H. had seven children.

George Eugene (1859 – 1927)

He was president of the Oliver China Works. With wife Cora and son Orville, George founded Sebring, Florida, in 1911.

Elizabeth (1836 – 1910) and George E. Sr. (1834 – 1915)

George and Elizabeth were married in 1856. They were the proud parents of these ten children.

Eva (1865 – 1956)

Mrs. (Rev.) J.H. Norris, of Pittsburgh, twin to Frank.

Emma (1872 – 1957)

Wife of C. J. Albright, treasurer for the Sebring Pottery.

Not pictured

Charles (1872 – 1877)

Charles died at age 5 of whooping cough.

The Sebring family, taken about 1890.

Left to right, back row: Will, Fred, Joseph, Oliver, Frank, Ellsworth.
Front row: George, Elizabeth, George Sr., Eva, and Emma.

Courtesy Sebring Historical Society, Sebring, Ohio.

The Ohio China Co., maker of Limoges Porcelain, East Palestine, OH, built c.1896.

Original postcard, publisher unknown, made in America. Earliest document showing the Limoges plant with logo.

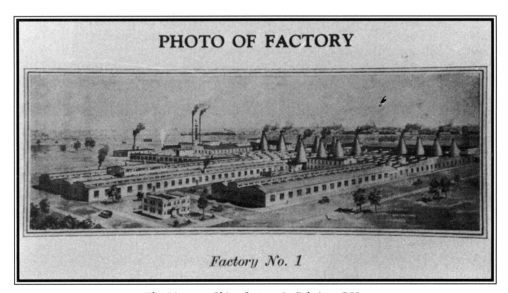

The Limoges China factory in Sebring, OH.

Photo from the company booklet *A Modern Story of the Worlds Most Ancient Art*, publisher unknown, c. 1930.

The Limoges China Co. in Sebring, OH.
Color postcard, date unknown. Courtesy Sebring Historical Society.

The following pages show the booklet
A Modern Story of the World's Most Ancient Art, c. 1930.
Courtesy Harrison Keller.

A MODERN STORY of the
WORLD'S
MOST ANCIENT ART

*A trip through
the Plant of the*
LIMOGES CHINA COMPANY
Sebring, Ohio

*C*OME WITH US through the pages of this little booklet. Be our special guest on a personally conducted word-picture tour of THE LIMOGES CHINA COMPANY'S factory at Sebring, Ohio.

We will try to make this both interesting and instructive, and at the end of the trip you will have a vivid mental picture of the fascinating process by which your beautiful chinaware set has come into existence.

The origin of pottery is obscured by the mists of antiquity. Long before metal working was conceived, when skins formed the only clothing known; preceding even the ancient discovery of fire, partially baked clay utensils were in common use.

Your chinaware set of delicate pattern and beautiful design, the artistic effort of the chemist and artisan of the present age, is but a modern adaptation of the primitive man's clay cup or earthen bowl.

This ancient lineage has brought pottery into the limelight of general interest because the his-

3

tory of the race has been written for centuries largely through fossils and pottery alone.

The action of heat on clay is truly remarkable. Just think; vessels so fragile that they crumble in the hands of the curior have endured for thousands of years withstanding atmospheric changes and chemical forces. Stone crumbles away, ink fades, paper decays, wood rots, but the earthen vessel survives and brings its message to us from long ages past.

Since history fails to inform us, we repeat for your information the legend, that modern potting traces its start to some pre-historic man, who more curious than his fellows, observed on a certain occasion the property of plastic clay to hold water in a hole made by the foot of some passing camel. The story further tells us that he conceived the idea that articles might be fashioned from this material, which would be more suitable to his wants than animal skins or the roughly hollowed gourds or stones—thus he became the first potter.

From this obscure beginning a great trade and art developed, affecting whole races. The early

4

secrets of pottery making were passed down through numerous families from father to son, and the potters were raised to a higher social plane than others of the clan or group.

Industry's Progress

After lying dormant for more than thirty centuries, the industry has taken tremendous strides forward within the last thirty years. Influenced by the demand for greater efficiency and lower costs, the potteries in the United States now represent the last word in up-to-the-minute manufacturing. The compounding of raw materials is no longer chance guess work, but is pre-determined by the ceramic chemist, power is employed in practically all processes, mechanical handling has been adopted, new machinery has been installed, and in the executive offices modern accounting and cost-finding methods are in common use.

The Limoges China Company

The Limoges China Company is a direct descendant of the chain of potteries, established by the five Sebring brothers, members of an old line of potters, at East Liverpool, Ohio, in 1887.

This infant plant soon outgrew its swaddling clothes and before long demanded room and op-

5

portunity, which the hills and ravines of picturesque East Liverpool could not supply. So in the late nineties a new location was sought, which would afford better living conditions for the employees and permit of plant expansion at a minimum expense. Such a site was found within four miles of Alliance, Ohio, and adjacent to Canton, Youngstown, Akron and Cleveland. Being planned and built as an ideal pottery center by the Sebring brothers, the town carries their name, and since its establishment in 1900 it has developed and prospered until now it has a population in excess of 5,000, most of whom work at the potteries. It possesses all modern improvements, including paved streets, efficient city government, excellent schools, good water, electric service and fire protection. It is in short, a typical high-class American community, and is always much admired by passing tourists.

Here in this thriving center in 1901 The LIMOGES CHINA COMPANY was formed by Mr. F. A. Sebring, one of the brothers, and today it operates as the largest principal unit of the combined Sebring units, one of the largest of its kind in the United States.

Sebring, Ohio, Is located almost equi-distant

6

between the two important cities of Cleveland and Pittsburgh. The main trunk line of the great Pennsylvania Railroad bisects the town and affords for The Limoges China Company and the other Sebring plants there the best possible facilities in rail transportation.

The Limoges China Company Product

Before entering the pottery, a few words about the product. As contrasted with the average imported dinnerware, which as a rule is vitreous and translucent, the beautiful product of The Limoges China Company and the average American pottery is classified by the United States Bureau of Standards as "semi-vitreous china-ware." This class of ware does not attempt competition with imported vitreous; nor does it have to since more than 80% of the ware gracing American tables is of the semi-vitreous type, known as porcerlain or semi-porcelain. A recent report from the United States Bureau of Standards reveals that semi-vitreous porcelain is far more durable than the imported vitreous ware, withstanding chipping, crazing and temperature change tests, which completely shattered or crazed all of the imported vitreous ware subjected to the same treatment. Attractive design, beauti-

7

ful decorations and low cost of semi-vitreous ware appeal to the average purchaser, and it has thereby become an indispensable commodity in the average American home.

Type of Plant

The Limoges China Company's plant and most of the other American potteries are of one story construction, built of brick, cement, and other fire-resisting materials. For an instant our attention is attracted by the many huge kiln chimneys, protruding through and extending above the roof of the plant, each belching forth smoke and fumes as the "firing" goes on within. The plant site covers ten and one-half acres of ground, and the working floor space is in excess of 125,000 square feet.

Trip Through the Plant

The plant is electrically equipped throughout except in the clay preparing processes for which the company manufactures its own power. We pass through the employee's entrance, and after winding our way through numerous departments arrive at the back of the plant, and here find the railroad siding on which is standing a string of cars.

8

Clay Bins

Raw Materials

Upon closer inspection we observe several car-loads of greyish blue material, and our guide informs us that this is a shipment of the imported English clay, which combined with other chemical elements forms the body of the semi-vitreous dinnerware. This clay is mined in the neighbor-hood of Devonshire, Wareham and Teigngrace, England, at a depth of sixty to eighty feet below

9

Weighing Clay

the surface. It is largely an aluminum-silicate composition, and in its preparation for chinaware manufacture, water, flint, spar, lime, magnesium and traces of other chemicals are added in proportions, pre-detrmined by the ceramic chemist on duty. Check tests are also run from time to time to see that the "batch" is right. This secret composition formula is the only trade secret in chinaware manufacture at the present time.

10

Extracting Water from Clay

In the meantime these car-loads of clay are being dumped in large out-door bins. The action of the rain and sunshine on the clay in this state acts as a purifying agent, so it is left here until ready for mixture and use.

Now workmen are attacking these large clay piles with shovels, loading the material into wheelbarrows and moving to the "mixing room," where according to the mixing formula it is weighed and

11

measured and then cast into huge mixers to be pulverized.

This all takes place in what is known as the "slip-house." Here after being ground fine, water is added in generous quantities, and the mixture leaves the "slip-house" in the form of very liquid mud. The solution then moves to the large filter presses where the water is again extracted and the clay mixture, now in the form of press cakes, is thrown upon a pile for tempering. Just prior to the extraction of the water by the filter presses, our guide points to the solution passing thinly over a flat steel surface, and we are told that this is a magnet which removes the tiny, microspocic particles of iron. Noticing our lack of comprehension, he further tells us that iron particles in the clay mixture are always a source of grief to the potter. In the intense heat of the kiln, the iron particles liquify and expand, producing a colored spot on the otherwise perfect ware.

After tempering the clay, in order to secure an average mixture, a section is sliced out in a large lump, lifted to the shoulders of a workman and put through the "pug mill," which suggests the old-fashioned sausage stuffer. After mixing the batch and once more adding water, the clay is

12

Jigger Wheel

made pliable for the worker. It is now ready to be formed into whatever type of piece is wanted.

Shaping the Pieces

A trolley carrier conveys the tempered, pliable clay mass to the "jigger line," a series of power operated potters' wheels. Here the helper pulls a handful of clay off the larger lump, and flattens it on his block by one blow of "the batter," a peculiarly shaped mallet, resembling a large,

13

The Green Room

round flat-iron. The thin, round pancake of clay is then slapped down over a plaster of paris mould shaped to form the inside of the plate, saucer or other flat piece. The mould is then fixed to the potter's wheel, the bottom of the piece being formed (as the wheel and mould revolve) by a stationary steel blade, shaped to the outline of the plate or other piece. Following this process, the shaped piece, without being removed from the

14

The Way Hollow Pieces are Shaped

mould, is put on a moving rack, and when the rack is full it goes into a heated drying room where it is revolved, thus replacing a rack full of freshly moulded ware by one carrying ware dry enough to handle.

15

Casting and Finishing

Removing Green Ware from the Mould

As the ware dries it shrinks 10% and loosens enough from the mould to make handling possible. Upon being removed from the mould, we pass to the finisher's bench" where the face of the ware is sponged, and the rough edges finished off. Next it is conveyed to the "green room" for further drying. In this state it is interesting to notice the workmen moving along rapidly and noiselessly,

16

balancing a board some four feet long on their heads, which is loaded with the green ware, piled on top of each other in inverted fashion. This is necessary since in this state the ware would disintegrate if handled mechanically.

The Way Hollow Pieces are Shaped

Differing entirely from the way in which the flat pieces of ware are made on the potter's wheel, all of the hollow pieces, such as pitchers, bowls and vegetable dishes, are moulded by hand. Plaster of paris is used for these moulds, the moulds being manufactured in a separate department of the pottery and then filled with a thin solution of clay. The plaster of paris draws the water out of the solution, leaving a thin coating of clay inside the mould. Silicate of soda and soda ash are found in this clay solution. Any excess of clay is then poured out, and after a brief drying period, the mould is opened, and the piece sent to the "green room" for final preparation before drying. Next handles, seperately moulded, are stuck to the cups, sugars, creams and covered dishes.

First Firing in Bisque Kiln

The dried, unfired ware is next carefully placed in fire resisting receptacles known as "saggers,"

17

Bisque Ware Room

these saggers or fire clay baskets filled with ware are sealed to prevent fumes and smoke of the kiln from coming in contact with the ware, and are then stacked on top of each other in the immense kiln until the kiln is filled or "placed." These kilns are dome shaped, converging at the top in the chimney from which the fumes and smoke escape. Furthermore these kilns, all of the intermittent type, are constructed of several thick-

18

Dipping

nesses of fire brick, reinforced by heavy steel bands, the diameter of their floor being some twenty feet and the altitude about eighteen feet.

After a kiln is stacked with ware, the door is sealed with bricks and reinforced with two steel

19

Placing Glost Kilns

bands. The heat is then introduced gradually from below, fuel being either natural gas or vaporized oil. The heat is slowly brought to a temperature of 2350 degrees Fahrenheit, and held there for forty-four hours after which the kiln is allowed to cool, equally slow. Upon being removed from this kiln the ware is called "biscuit" or "bisque." It is now semi-vitrified, or partly glass formed and although still porous, has the "ring" and strength of the finished product.

20

We now find that it is conveyed to the bisque room where it is brushed, stamped with a trade mark, dressed and prepared for the next process. It then goes to the "dipping room" where the "dippers" take each piece separately and dip it into the glaze material. The glaze very much resembles a tub of average strength white wash. After being immersed, the piece is allowed to dry on racks, and then again placed in the "saggers" for the second or "glost" firing. In being put into the "saggers" for this second firing each piece is separated from the others by pins, protruding from the sides of the "saggers," and as we examine some of the ware which has come from the glost kilns, we observe several small glass like blotches on the bottom of each piece. These are places where the pieces have rested on these tiny triangular "sagger pins," and in the intense heat of the kiln as the glaze liquifies, it runs and gathers in a tiny globule around each of the supporting pins. When the ware is lifted from the pins, this drop of solidified glaze is destroyed, leaving the little blotch in each piece on the bottom of the piece. These tiny blotches do NOT represent defects in the ware as many people imagine, this being characteristic of all ware, and

21

Glost Ware Room

impossible to eliminate in the manufacturing process.

Dressing and Grading White Ware

If these tiny globules or projections of solidified glaze, left by the china pins are not destroyed as the piece is removed, they are cut off by the stroke of a file in the "dressing room." The "dressing room" also serves as the "grading room." At this point all the white ware is graded into firsts

22

Decalcomania

and seconds, but the grading does not stop here; the pile of firsts is then graded into "selects" and firsts and the seconds are in turn graded into seconds and thirds, the firsts being the lower half of the original firsts and the thirds the lower half of the original seconds — thus we find the four grades: SELECTS, FIRSTS, SECONDS, THIRDS.

After being graded we find that the ware is stored in racks in the stock room until such time

23

as a supply shall be withdrawn for decorating. The stock room is immense and acts as the main storage point in the whole operation. Some idea of its capacity can be gained from the statement that at all times, the company has something over five millions of dishes in this department alone.

24

Lining

How the Ware is Decorated

One of the biggest factors in lowering china-ware costs was the invention and substitution of "decalcomania" for the slow tedious hand painting work formerly used. Now practically all medium

25

Tunnel Kiln, General View

priced dinnerware, and much of the expensive kind, is decorated by this transfer process.

Most of us recall the transfer colored picture papers of childhood, which we eagerly purchased with every stray cent and after moistening the paper, with great delight we transferred the print to the backs of our hands and arms, or perhaps "dressed up" our picture books.

The decalcomania print closely resembles the

26

Tunnel Kiln Car

picture prints of our chiildhood fancy, and the transfer process is much the same, except that the print in this case is composed of analine dyes and the paper is a special variety, paying an excellent royalty to the inventor.

The ware to be decorated is withdrawn from the storage room and conveyed to the decorating department, which is manned or perhaps we should say "womanned" largely by girls, many of

27

Decorated Ware Room, Showing Selection and wrapping of ware

whom are highly skilled. Baskets of the ware to be decorated are set near a large revolving table, one worker gives the dish a coat of sizing or adhesive where the print is to be applied. The piece then moves through a drying oven and is taken off for the application of the design.

After this is applied and rubbed well, the dish passes through a mechanical washer which re-

28

Packing Department, showing packing of barrels and wrapped ware

moves the paper backing, is dried mechanically and made ready for the color lining and gold band work, which is all done by hand. It is interesting to note with what deft skill the young ladies at the "lining tables" do their work. Holding a small lining brush in her right hand, which is station-ary, a girl will whirl the plate, cup or saucer on a revolving disc, and more rapidly than it can be

29

General View of Stock Room

described, a delicate color line or gold band is run around the piece, perfectly balanced with the rest of the design. Still others do the gold handle work on a piece which requires a real artistic touch.

30

After a suitable drying period the ware is conveyed to the decorating kiln for the third and final firing.

"Fired" in the Decorating Kiln

Because of the great saving of time and effort, the decalcomania process has brought quality chinaware within the financial reach of the average American family. But this is not the only advantage. In the decorating kiln the temperature is raised to more than 1500 degrees Fahrenheit. This intense heat causes the analine oils and color bands of the decoration completely to fuse into the piece, thus becoming absolutely indestructible, and the full beauty and lustre of the delicate shading lasts as long as the piece is used. On the other hand much of the hand painted china will fade or erase in time, subjected as dishes are to washing and friction.

Special Type af Decorating Kiln

The decorting kiln at The Limoges China Company is one of the most modern machines in the industry. In sharp contrast to the laborious and time-consuming process by which the kiln of the intermittent type is filled by hand, sealed, fired, cooled, and then again emptied by workers, the Limoges China Company operates a continuous

31

tunnel type of decorating kiln, the complete operation of which is under the direction and control of one man. Here the ware is racked up on cars, built of fire-resisting material which move on a steel track in a continuous mechanical cycle. One car with ware to be fired, enters one end of the tunnel kiln each twelve minutes, thereby pushing out at the other end a truck filled with the completely fired ware. This is a perpetual process and is outstandingly efficient.

From the kilns the ware moves to the decorated ware room where once more it is carefully inspected and graded, after which it goes to the shipping department.

Packing and Shipping of Product

Here orders are filled, and sent to the packing room where a small army of journeymen pack the ware in barrels, boxes and cartons, nesting the pieces in between thick layers of straw.

We are now back at the rear of the plant, near the point where we first observed the unloading of the clay. At this point your chinaware set and the ware of your many American neighbors is loaded directly into Pennsylvania line cars and sent speeding on its way to some destination lying

32

in that great expanse bounded by Canada, the Gulf of Mexico and the two oceans.

Behind every effect there is a cause, and so our journey would not be complete without a brief stop in the main offices, where we meet the directing heads of this vast enterprise.

A pleasure awaits us here as we meet Mr. F. A. Sebring, a gentleman of charming and gracious manner, who founded this great organization in 1901, and who still remains active in the direction of its operation.

He has surrounded himself with a corps of efficient associates, all of whom share responsibilities in this great undertaking.

In addition to The Limoges China Company, through which we have just passed, Mr. F. A. Sebring is the directing head of four other large potteries. The F. A. Sebring potteries command an enviable reputation in the ceramic world—being the recognized leaders in this field, both from a standpoint of production and for the originality and distinctiveness of their products.

33

And now good-bye. We are glad to have had you as our guests and we hope this "word-tour" has been interesting as well as enlightening. Until such time as we can welcome you to the plant in person, we shall dare to indulge the hope that your dinnerware set, each piece of which is the result of some three hundred and thirty-three hand operations, will hold for you a beauty and a charm not hitherto possible.

34

The Limoges office staff.
Top center: Mabel Reynolds (mother of Mrs. Ball). Others unknown. Photo taken in 1903 or 1905. Courtesy Francis Ball.

The Limoges foreman family picnic.
Silver Park, Aug. 13, 1947. Photo courtesy Sebring Historical Society.

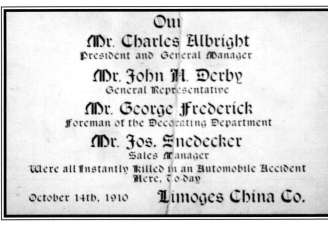

Black Friday, October 14, 1910.
Obituary card, courtesy Eleanor Yaggi.

BLACK FRIDAY

THE LIMOGES CHINA CO. TOP MANAGEMENT:

Mr. Charles Albright, President and General Manager
Mr. John M. Derby, General Representative
Mr. George Frederick, Foreman of the Decorating Department
Mr. Joseph Snedecker, Sales Manager

Were all instantly killed in an automobile accident on October 14, 1910. The accident occurred at the Naylors Crossing, Sebring, OH, with the Stack Electric Train enroute to East Liverpool, OH. Mr. Charles Albright was married to Emma Sebring.

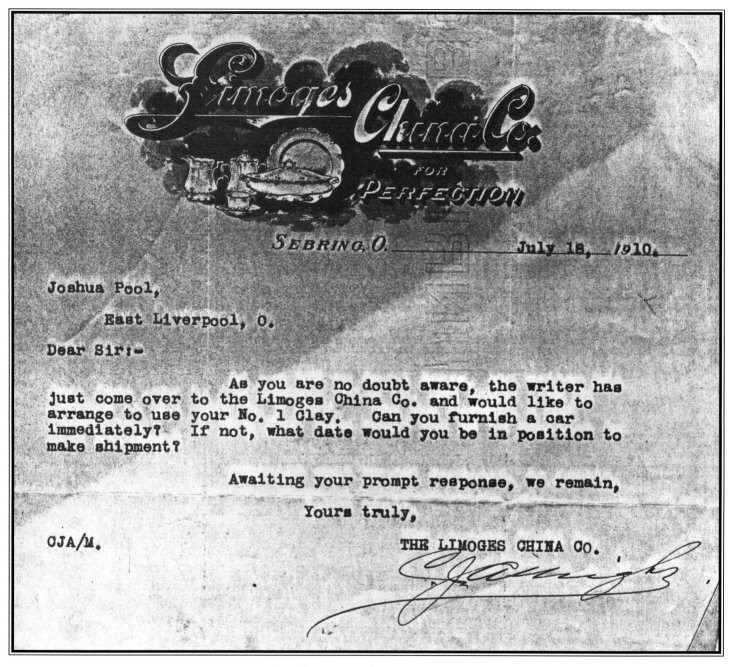

Letter from the Limoges China Co., July 18, 1910.

Pin tray.
Promotional item, company logo in white and yellow. 5" x 2¾".

Limoges plant in 1991.

Flyer, 1943 promotion for National Bouquet (top left, page 135).

Oct. 9, 1928.

Des. 76,557

F. A. SEBRING

PLATE OR SIMILAR ARTICLE

Filed July 8, 1927

Fig. 1

Fig. 2

Fig. 3

Inventor

Frank A. Sebring

By

Frease and Bond   Attorneys

Patent (bottom left, page 84).

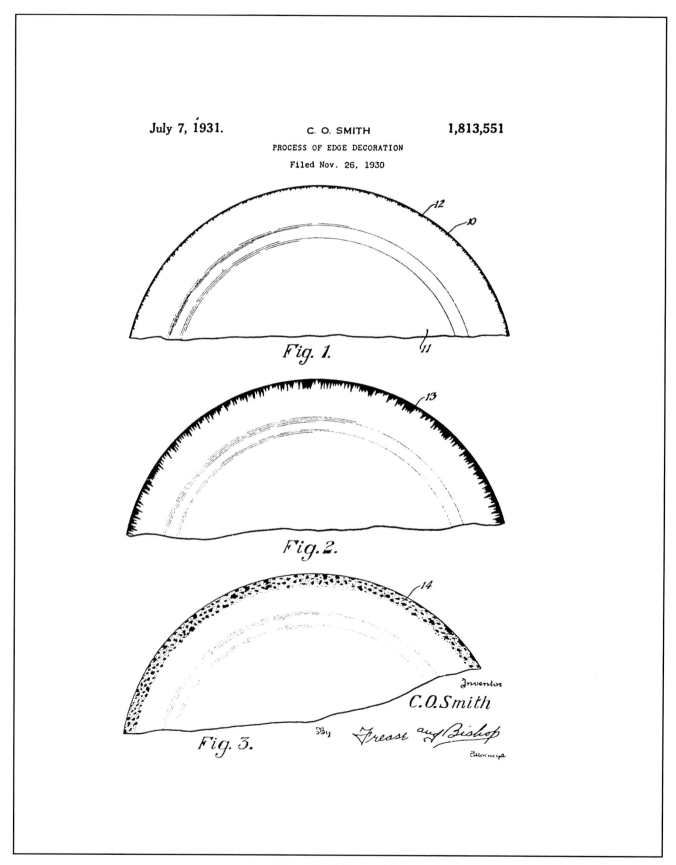

Patent (top left, page 84).

Advertisement, September 1940, *China, Glass & Lamps*, Vol. 60 #1 (page 107).

AMERICAN LIMOGES CHINA INC.

FOUNDED 1904
SPONSORS THIS SPACE IN HONOR OF THE

CLASS OF 1940

Quenten Ballantyne	Opal Carrier
Lewis Bandy	Mildred Christ
Ralph Beck	Grace Clunen
Roger Briggs	Doris Davies
Willard Briggs	Mary Demark
William Brown	Olympia Dragimir
John Brunt	Dorothy Dunlap
Joe Choma	Mildred Eells
Winfield Clatterbuck	Evelyn Green
William Cope	Margie Hughes
James Deonise	Merle Iddings
Elmer Hoff	Violette Jordan
John Fahnert	Clara Kirksey
Paul Gednetz	Loretta Kniseley
Gene Haberland	Mildred Lewis
James Herren	Edith Luginbuhl
Carl Hillary	Mary Mallernee
Floyd Hoopes	Hazel Malysa
Sam Hutmacher	Martha Manning
James Kilbreath	Mary Manos
James King	Dolores Mellor
Robert Class	Ginger Michael
Robert Meek	Mary Morris
Richard Myers	Minnie Morrison
Cletus Nezbeth	Adeline Murphy
Ralph Pinkerton	Betty Nestor
Wesley Pollock	Lucile Ostermeier
John Reynolds	Nora Parr
Robert Walker	Erla Paulin
Harry Surls	Laura Peterson
George Whinery	Florence Pope
Don Elliot	Dolores Sanderson
Betty Ailes	Johann Slavin
Helen Ailes	Sara Snyder
Aluce Albright	Imogene Sutton
Florence Amabeli	Margaret Ward
Neva Baird	June Watson
Eleanor Barclay	Virginia Welce
Jean Barcus	Kathryn Wilson
Doris Brock	Pearl Wogon
Dorlene Brubaker	Dorothy Woolf
Martha Campbell	Betty Yarian
Doris Frye	

MANUFACTURERS OF NATIONALLY-KNOWN PRODUCTS

1940 Sebring High School yearbook, page 108.

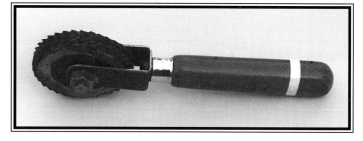

Decorating wheel.
Made of rubber, it was dipped in gold and used to make patterns on wares. Owned by Mary Baker who was a decorator at the Limoges Co. for more than 20 years. Courtesy Howard Baker.

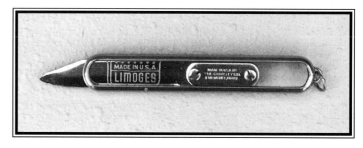

Pocket knife with retractable blade.
Promotional item with the company logo. Made by the Christy Co., Fremont, Ohio. Patented.

THE WARES

SHAPES

Shape is the style of the greenware before decorating.

ALARA
AMERICANA 1934
CANDELIGHT
CASINO . . . . .playing cards shape
COLONIAL
CORINTHIAN . . .fluted edge
DIANA 1934
GLAMOUR . . . . . .very plain
HEXAGON . . . . . .early shape, 7-sided plates
JIFFY . . . . .1935 refrigerator ware, modern shape
MANHATTAN . . .1934
NEW YORKER . .1953
PURITAN . . . . . . .early shape
REGENCY
RIPPLE EDGE . . .patented
SEBRING
SQUARE . . . . .used mostly with Peach Blow Pink glazing
SWIRL
TRIUMPH . . . . . . .horizontal lines, design by Viktor Schreckengost
VICTORY . . . . . . .vertical lines (made for Salem China)

DECOR

The line is the style of decoration.

The same decal used with a different trim or on a different shape, will have a different name. It is often part of the backstamp.

BURGUNDY . . . . .dark red trim
COTILLION . . . . .pastel color rim
DUSTITONE . . . . .very light pastel
EMERALD GLOW . . . .bright green glazing
FOREST GREEN . . . . . .dark green edge
GOLDEN GLOW . . . . . .yellow glazing
IMPERIAL . . . . .small gold lace trim on beige rim
MANDARIN . . . . .light olive green trim
MAROON EMPEROR .wide gold lace trim on darker rim
MONSOON . . . . .color feathered edge with or
                          without design
MOOD . . . . .shades of the same color on edge
PEACH BLOW . . . . .pink color glazing
PREMIER . . . . .several gold lines on beige rim
ROYAL . . . . .wide gold lace on beige rim
SURF . . . . .two-color border on Triumph shape
VISTA . . . . .color on Triumph shape (assorted colors)
WISHMAKER . . . . .color trim

PATTERNS

Notes: An asterisk (*) denotes that the pattern was named by the author. The name was not known at the time of print-ing. Some patterns were not named but were referred to by the decal or catalog number; others may have more than one name depending on the decor or the trim.

The spelling of the pattern name may differ from one piece to another, even if it is the same decor. At one time the Limoges China and the Sebring companies were sister plants. Some pieces were made in one plant, some in the other. Within one set, some plates may bear the Limoges stamp, the platter have the Sebring stamp, and the saucers have no stamp at all.

Over the span of more than 50 years, many other manu-facturers used the same decals and copied off each other, whatever the style of the moment. When looking for matching pieces, it is important to realize that time and use may have changed the colors and the trim.

Any corrections and additions to this list are welcome.

CARE OF DISHES

Limoges dishes should *not* go in the dishwasher.

Hand wash with comfortably hot water and mild soap, then rinse. Drying with a soft dishcloth is best to prevent water spots, especially if the water is hard or contains a lot of minerals. The greatest care should be given to cups, as handles break easily. Round paper coffee filters, placed between the dishes, are an inexpensive way to prevent damage. When not used for long periods of time, the dishes can be stored safely in pretty cookie tins with paper towels. They are always ready for the table.

PRICE

The prices listed in this book are only to be used as a guide.

They are retail prices, the average amount of money one can expect to pay in a collector's or antique shop for an item in reasonably good condition — prices we have seen, prices we have paid, or would be willing to pay. It does not include the 50¢ price tag for a sugar bowl without handles sold at a flea market, although we have seen such an item at $5.00. Nor does it include a dealer at a large antique & collectible show asking $300.00 for a platter (Triumph shape with decals by American Limoges), thinking it was hand-painted French porcelain. These are extremes.

Value, like beauty, is often in the eye of the beholder. Grandmother's dishes have sentimental value beyond price. They are part of someone's heritage and memories of family gatherings, around the table with good food and happy times.

Fair market value is the cold business of dollars and cents. Grandmother's set, in a fancy shop on Main Street or waiting in a dusty antique mall, are only pieces of pottery. Their worth decided by the fickle laws of trading.

STEED*, mark 3, vase 12", front, hand-painted roses, not signed, very rare, Gloria Limoges collection. $150.00.

STEED*, mark 3, vase, back view.

SOUVENIR ST. LOUIS EXPO 1904, mark 1, bowl 7", decal on luster, Palace Of Machinery. $45.00 – 50.00.

NORTHWOODS*, mark 3, plate 7" sq., folded handkerchief corners, stream in forest decal on green luster. Advertising Winkler's Chocolates. $75.00 – 85.00.

CALENDAR 1909, mark 1, plate 7", holly and calendar decal with gold edge. Gold stamp: Ft Wayne, Ind. $30.00 – 40.00.

CALENDAR 1909, mark 1, plate 7", holly and calendar decal with pink border. In gold letters: "Compliments of M.A. Burnes — Complete House Furnishing, Woburn, Mass." $35.00 – 40.00.

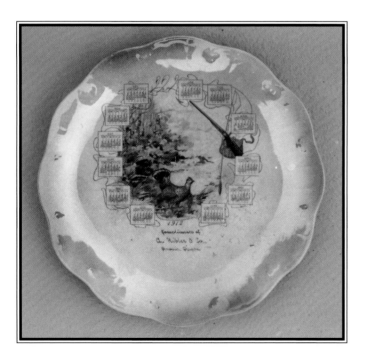

CALENDAR 1912, mark 3, plate 8", hunting scene decal on luster. "Compliments of A. Nibler & Co, Gervais, Oregon," in gold letters. $35.00 – 45.00.

CALENDAR 1913, mark 3, plate 8", airplane with landscape decal, flow blue border with gold lace edge. In gold letters: "Wholesale & Retail. D. Bozzollo, Prop. 300 2nd Ave So. Seattle." $45.00 – 50.00.

CALENDAR 1915, mark 3, plate 7" sq., decal on green, baby & old man with calendar on scroll. Ann Gorin-Kellner collection. $45.00 – 50.00.

CALENDAR 1915, mark 3A, plate 8", Panama Canal map with small calendars in a circle. Flow blue with gold edge. Gold letters on back: "Hedberg Brothers Shoe Store Tacoma, Wash." $30.00 – 35.00.

OLD GLORY, mark 3, plate 8", decal map of Panama Canal with a ring of 27 presidents. Green edge with gold lace. Ed Banks collection. $35.00 – 40.00.

OLD GLORY, mark 3, plate 9", decal map of Panama Canal encircled by ring of presidents. Flow blue edge with gold lace. Gold stamp front: "Compliments Of N. Olson 1621 8th Ave No. Minneapolis, Minn." $35.00 – 40.00.

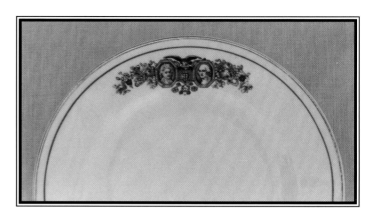

LINDBERG 1927, mark 17, plate 8½" sq., portrait of Col. Lindberg, Spirit of St. Louis, New York to Paris commemorative, with ring of red poppies on yellow glazing. $75.00 – 95.00.

WASHINGTON*, mark 17, plate 5", floral and medallions around the likenesses George and Martha Washington are encircled by one blue and one gold line. The eagle, wishbone, four leaf clover, swastika, and horseshoe were good luck symbols in 1932. Moyer collection. $25.00.

BLOOMBERG*, mark 32, plate 10", souvenir plate with pink and gold trim. "An Invitation To 50th Birthday Party For Harry Bloomberg, Waldorf Astoria, June 3rd, 1947, 7:30 PM." He was president of the Limoges China Co. at the time. $100.00.

MINNESOTA WOODS*, ashtray 5", stream in forest decal, flow blue edge. Souvenir: "NARD Aug. 20th – Sept. 4th 1915. Minneapolis, Minn." On back: "Compliments of the Limoges China Co. of Sebring O. Originators of the 'Direct to you' advertising plan." Same ashtrays with assorted designs and slogans used in advertising. $40.00 – 45.00.

AMERICAN LIMOGES, mark 80, pin tray 3" sq., gold letters on Peach Blow pink, "Compliments of American Limoges China Co. Sebring — Ohio USA." $25.00.

SUNSET HILL*, no mark, ashtray 6¼" white with gold letters. Souvenir "Convention Sunset Hill House Sept. 19 – 20. Independent Food & Grocers New Hampshire. American Limoges China Corp. Mfg. Potters Sebring Ohio. James L. Mahony Executive Secretary Phone 5-7781." On back: "Samuel J Davidson Boston Mass. Factory Representative." $35.00.

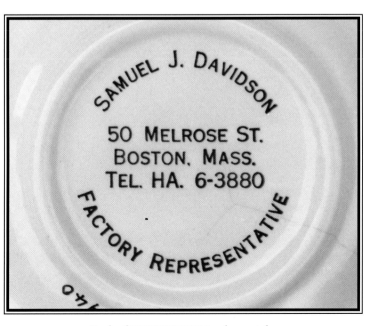

Back of SUNSET HILL, above right.

PORTLAND FRUITS*, mark 3, platter 10", fruits and flowers decal on luster, on back in gold letters: "A—Reminder of Haradon's Tru-Fruit Chocolates, Portland, Oregon." $40.00 – 45.00.

APPLE LYNNVILLE*, mark 5, plate 7", decal with three red apples in center, maroon trim, gold letters: "Lynnville IA." $20.00 – 25.00.

IOWA PEACHES*, mark 3, plate 7", three peaches with foliage in center, maroon trim on edge. "Souvenir, Denver Iowa," in gold letters. $20.00 – 25.00.

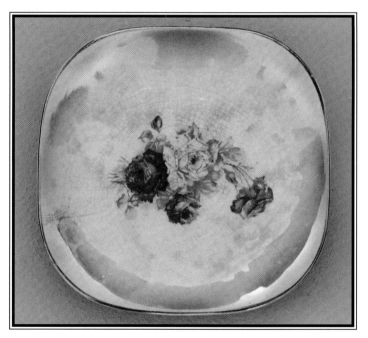

RIVERSIDE COTTAGES*, mark 3, plate 7½", landscape decal, maroon trim on edge, gold letters on front: "Souvenir of El Dorado, Kansas." $20.00 – 25.00.

ROSE GARDEN*, mark 18, plate 7¾" sq., roses on luster, on back in gold letters: "Smith Baldwin Co. Opening 1926 Mineral Ridge Ohio." $25.00 – 30.00.

GUYEAU ROSES*, mark 3, plate 8¼", yellow roses, gold lace trim on edge. Decal signed GUYEAU. Gold stamp on back: "Compliments of the Season 1914 — C F Wiebush." $25.00 – 30.00.

BLUE BELLS*, mark 18, platter 7½", three floral decals with blue rim, on back with gold letters: "Compliments of National Furn. Co. 314 E. Main St. Alliance Ohio." $25.00.

GABRIELLE*, mark 3, plate 7½", roses decal, maroon trim. Souvenir. $25.00.

GABRIELLE*, mark 3, plate 7½", roses decal, maroon trim. Souvenir. $25.00.

GRIST MILL*, mark 3, plate 7", landscape decal, gold and green trim. "Compliments of Centerville, Iowa." Watkins collection. $30.00 – 35.00.

AKRON MUMS*, mark 51, platter 9", yellow and orange floral decal on lower front, in gold letters: "1937 Season's Greetings, R.W. Schumacker Coffee Inc. 268 S. Main St. Akron, Ohio." $30.00 – 35.00.

CLEVELAND*, mark 31, platter 11", pink floral center, gold lettered advertisement: "The South Side Department Store, Professor and Jefferson Ave. Cleveland, Ohio." $30.00 – 35.00.

CEDAR POINT*, mark 28, 1946, plate 7¼", souvenirs made for the "Lake Shore Pioneer Chapter New York Central Veterans, Cedar Point, Ohio." Many different designs were made, not all by the Limoges China Co. $20.00 – 25.00.

CEDAR POINT, mark 32, 1950, petit point design. $20.00 – 25.00.

CEDAR POINT, mark 38, 1954, Currier & Ives winter scene. $20.00 – 25.00.

CEDAR POINT, mark 38, 1955, Eiffel Tower. $20.00 – 25.00.

AMERICAN LEGION, mark 58, plate 6½", Post 166, gold logo with blue trim. Courtesy Post 166, Alliance, OH. $10.00.

DAUGHTERS OF AMERICA, mark 67, plate 10", logo with gold lace trimmed edge. $10.00.

REFORMED CHURCH, mark 17, plate 6¼", gold letters and two gold lines on rim, on back "6 31." City and state unknown. $8.00 – 10.00.

PASSING FANCY, mark 3, plate 10", horse and rider at the well by Heywood Hardy. $30.00 – 35.00.

MONOGRAM*, mark 34, plate 9¼", single letter "G" in gold with fine gold line on edge. Made with all letters. $8.00 – 10.00.

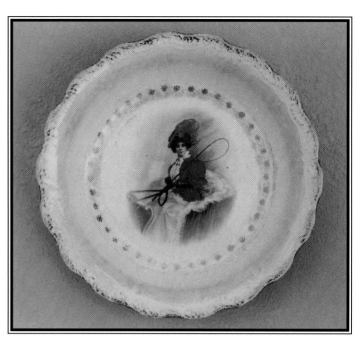

ANGELIQUE*, mark 3A, plate 9½", portrait of a lady with long hair on white with gold trim. $60.00.

HELEN*, mark 3, bowl 8½", portrait of a lady with a red hat with gold trim. $45.00 – 50.00.

MAYBELLE*, mark 3, plate 9", portrait of a lady with purple plumes, on luster with serpentine trim. Courtesy of Carnaby. $30.00 – 35.00.

IDA*, mark 1, plate 11", portrait of a lady in blue, gold lace trim. Watkins collection. $30.00 – 35.00.

SARAH*, mark 3A, plate 10", portrait of a lady with green plume hat. $30.00 – 35.00.

MONA*, no mark, plate 7½", portrait of a lady with horse on white leaf and green luster. $25.00 – 30.00.

GLADYS*, mark 3A, plate 9½", portrait of a lady on luster. $35.00 – 40.00.

QUEEN LOUISE*, mark 3, plate 10", portrait of Louise of Mecklemberg, wife of Frederik III of Prussia. Flow blue with gold lace edge. Also 1910 calendar plate, mark 3, a popular design used by many companies. $35.00 – 40.00.

MANDA IN MAROON, mark 55, plate 9", official portrait of HSM Queen Elizabeth by Allen Hughes, June 2, 1953. K-S220 CD. $30.00 – 35.00.

MARY, no mark, plate 10", large center decal. Wide gold lace on cobalt blue rim. Also made with red border. Howard Baker collection. $20.00 – 25.00.

RIVERSIDE COTTAGES*, mark 3A, bowl 9", landscape decal, gold trim. Same decor also made on luster. $30.00 – 35.00.

SPRING FLIGHT*, mark 3, bowl 9", flock of birds, white with gold trim. $30.00 – 35.00.

SPRING FLIGHT*, no mark, plate 9½", flock of birds with pink flowers, white star on luster. $25.00 – 30.00.

PEACHIE*, mark 18, bowl 8¼", center fruit decal on luster. $25.00 – 30.00.

SUNRIPE*, mark 3, plate 10", large decal of three apples in center on luster. On back in gold letters: "Stark Bros., 1889 – 1909, 20th Anniversary Clarion Iowa." $25.00 – 30.00.

FRUITLAND*, mark 3, plate 10", large fruit decal on luster. $35.00 – 40.00.

DELICIOUS*, mark 3, bowl 9", large decal with three apples in center, gold edge trim. Similar pattern with green edge on oval platter. $25.00 – 30.00.

SANTA ROSA*, mark 3A, platter 12", large plums with foliage, gold lace trim. Very ornate blank. $30.00 – 35.00.

MUSCATEL*, mark 5, plate 7¼", white grapes and foliage on gray luster. $20.00 – 25.00.

BORDEAUX*, mark 3, plate 10", colorful grapes in center, green border. $20.00 – 25.00.

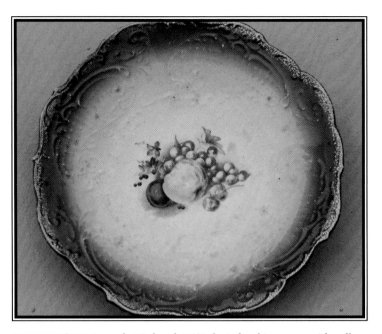

FRUIT BOWL*, mark 3C, bowl 11½", fruit decal in center with yellow and green, gold edge. Very colorful. $45.00 – 50.00.

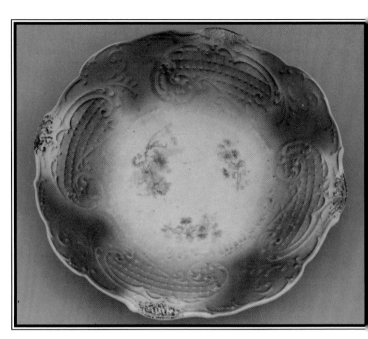

FLOWER BOWL*, mark 3A, bowl 11½", same shape as fruit bowl three small floral decals, pink and green trim. $45.00 – 50.00.

ROMANCE*, mark 1, plate 9½", large pink roses and violets decal in center, gold lace on scalloped edge. $18.00 – 20.00.

SPRING BOUQUET*, mark 3, plate 10", large decal of roses and lilacs, gold lace edge on flow blue. Same pattern on 7" plate. $35.00 – 40.00.

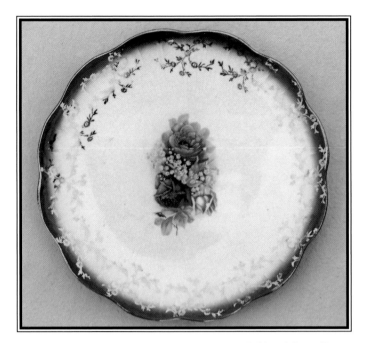

JUNE BRIDE*, mark 3, plate 7½", roses with lily of the valley in center, flow blue and gold lace trim. Made in other sizes. $25.00 – 30.00.

ROSY*, mark 3, plate 9½", three roses in center, flow blue with gold swags on edge. $35.00 – 40.00.

ROSY*, mark 3, platter 11½", three roses in center, flow blue with gold swags on edge. $50.00 – 60.00.

MARGARET*, mark 3, plate 8", small violets and daisies in center, flow blue with gold swags on rim. $30.00 – 35.00.

WIND-MOLEN*, mark 3, plate 9½", small blue windmill in center, flow blue and gold swags on rim. $30.00 – 35.00.

BLUE MUMS*, mark 3, plate 9½", small blue floral design in center, gold trim on flow blue edge. $30.00 – 35.00.

HEATHER*, mark 3, plate 9½", blue edge with delicate gold trim in center and on border. $30.00 – 35.00.

BOOK'S PEAR*, mark 3, bowl 8", pear in center, flow blue edge. On back, in gold letters: "Book's Cut the Price on Good Shoes, 206 South Market St., Canton, Ohio." $35.00 – 40.00

WESTERN*, mark 3, bowl 8", cattle at the river decal, gold trimmed flow blue trellis edge. $25.00 – 30.00.

TRELLIS BLUE*, mark 3, bowl 8", flow blue and gold rim. $25.00 – 30.00.

FRIENDEN*, no mark, bowl 6", children in traditional Dutch costumes in center, flow blue and gold rim. $20.00 – 25.00.

FLOW BLUE*, mark 5, bowl 8½", gold lace edge on flow blue rim on white. Scalloped raised edge. $18.00 – 20.00.

COLONIAL BLUE*, mark 18, bowl 5½", white with gold swags on flow blue rim dated 9-23. Puritan shape. $18.00 – 20.00.

BLUE SCALLOPS*, mark 3, plate 7¼", Colonial shape, flow blue rim on raised border. $15.00 – 18.00.

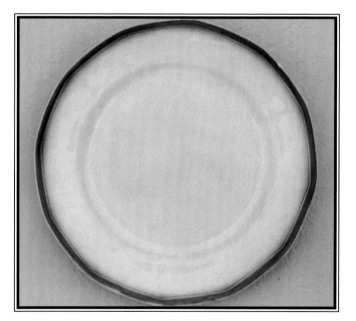

FLOW BLUE*, mark 18, plate 7", colonial shape, blue rim on white, 11-24. $15.00 – 18.00.

FLOW BLUE*, mark 18, plate 6", Puritan shape, white with gold lace on flow blue. Numbers under plate 9-23. $15.00 – 18.00.

FLOW BLUE*, mark 18, dish, gold swag design on flow blue rim. This dish has lost its cover. $10.00.

FAHNERT*, no mark, coffee pot, white with flow blue c. 1905. C. E. Fahnert was an officer of the Limoges China Co. in the early days. John Fahnert collection. $150.00.

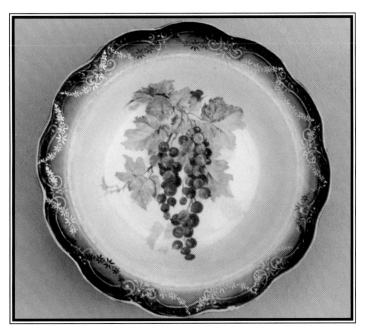

CURRANTS*, mark 3, bowl 10", large red currants in center with brown and gold lace edge. $65.00 – 70.00.

CHERRIES*, mark 3, plate 7", cherries and gooseberries in center with gold lace on green border. $15.00 – 20.00.

GRAPES*, mark 3, plate 7" hex., purple grapes and foliage center with gold lace edge on green border. $15.00 – 20.00.

GRAPES*, mark 3A, plate 10" hex., purple grapes with foliage, gold designs on green rim. $25.00 – 30.00.

KENT*, mark 3, plate 7", fruit decal in center with gold lace trim on green border. Melon and other fruits within a set. $15.00 – 20.00.

ANNABELLE*, mark 3, plate 7", violets and snowballs center, gold lace edge on green. $15.00 – 20.00.

ISABELLE*, mark 3, plate 7", roses and snowballs in center, gold lace edge on green. $15.00 – 20.00.

ERIN*, mark 5, plate 7", raspberries and flowers in center, gold lace edge on green. $15.00 – 20.00.

COUNTRY ROSE*, mark 3, plate 7", pink roses, gold lace trim on green. $15.00 – 20.00

PORTLAND ROSE*, mark 3, plate 7", pink moss roses in center, gold lace edge on green. $15.00 – 20.00.

COUNTESS OF LIMOGES*, mark 3, plate 10", large roses in shades of pink in center, gold lace edge on green. $25.00 – 35.00.

JUNE BRIDE*, mark 3A, plate 10", roses and lily of the valley in center, gold lace edge on green. Same pattern in flow blue. $25.00 – 35.00.

SPRING JOY*, mark 3, plate 10", large pink roses with white blossoms in center, gold lace edge on green. $25.00 – 35.00.

YELLOW ROSES*, mark 3, plate 7", large yellow roses in center, gold lace edge on green. $15.00 – 20.00.

MERRY MAY*, mark 18, plate 10", roses and lily of the valley in center on luster. $25.00 – 35.00.

ALEXANDRA*, mark 18, plate 10", roses and snowballs center on luster. 12-33. $25.00 – 35.00.

MIMI*, no mark, bowl 9½", floral decal in center, gold swags on green edge. $25.00 – 35.00.

SWEET ROSE*, mark 18, plate 10", pink and white rose center decal on luster. $10.00 – 15.00.

THERESA*, mark 17, platter 11", center rose decal on luster. $10.00 – 15.00.

POPPY ALITE*, mark 3A, plate 8¼", red poppy in center inside white leaf on green luster with gold trim. Decal signed Alite. $25.00 – 30.00.

OLD DUTCH WINDMILL, mark 20, plate 8½", scallop edge. Windmill decal, no trim. Same decor on Victory shape by Salem. $8.00 – 10.00.

BLANCHE*, mark 18, plate 5", all white Colonial shape, 11-24. $5.00.

BLUE BIRD, mark 18, serving dish 10½", blue bird on sprig of pink flowers, blue line on edge. A very popular pattern in the early 1900s. $50.00 – 60.00.

PURITAN, mark 9, coupe soup 8", gold filet on white. 1910 – 35. $5.00 – 10.00.

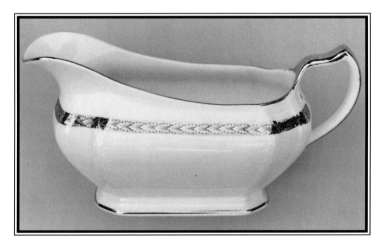

PLATINUM LEAF, mark 17, gravy 7½", silver trim on white. Stamped "15 Pennyweight Platinum 11 29." $25.00.

PLATINUM LEAF, mark 17, coffee pot, silver trim on white. V. Watkins collection. $50.00.

GOLD LEAF*, mark 17, butter dish 9¼" with cover, ribbon of leaves on gold rim. $45.00.

GOLD LEAF*, no mark, cup and saucer 5", ribbon of leaves on gold trim. $10.00 – 15.00.

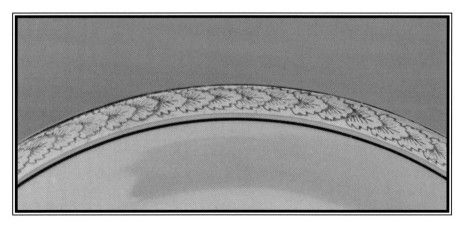

GOLD LEAF*, mark 17, some pieces mark 8, plate 9", ribbon of leaves on gold trim, stamp 7, pattern close-up. $10.00 – 12.00.

ETCHED GOLD, mark 35, cup and saucer, small leaves on gold ribbon. $10.00 – 15.00.

BELVEDERE, mark 51, plate 7", etched gold trim on white, 22K gold, 1948. $5.00 – 7.00

BURNISH GOLD, mark 20, plate 6", fine black line and gold edge on Ivory Ware. Some pieces with mark 18. $5.00 – 7.00

BURNISH GOLD, mark 17, gravy boat 8½", fine black line and gold trim. $15.00 – 20.00.

GOLD RING*, mark 3, sugar bowl with cover, gold trim on white. $20.00 – 25.00.

GOLD RING*, mark 3, butter dish with cover, gold trim on white. $35.00.

HOLLYWOOD, mark 61, bowl 6", two gold bands on white, 1934. $5.00 – 7.00.

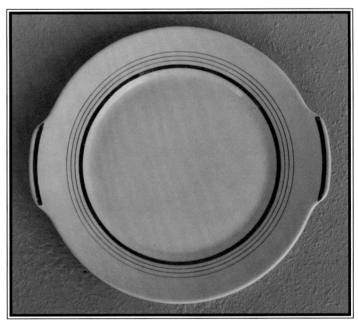

SILVER AGE, mark 60, platter 11", 22K white gold rings on white. $15.00.

SILVER AGE, mark 61, coffee server 9" tall with cover, white gold rings on white. $35.00 – 40.00.

SILVER AGE, no mark, salt and pepper shakers, white gold rings on white. $8.00 – 12.00 pair.

RITZ PLATINUM, mark 30, platter 11½", seven silver rings on pink Peach Blow. (Shown with creamer.) $25.00.

RITZ PLATINUM, mark 30, cup and saucer, seven silver rings on pink Peach Blow. $10.00 – 15.00.

30 KGFE, mark 56, plate 9¾", silver feather edge, one silver line. $5.00 – 7.00.

PLATINUM BRACELET, mark 32, platter 12", silver garland on rim Courtesy Nancy Pate. $20.00 – 25.00.

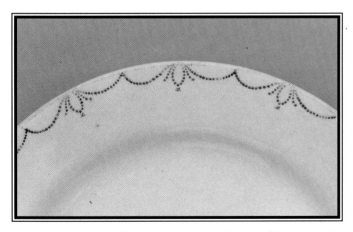

GOLD STARS*, mark 5, plate 9", swags of tiny gold stars on rim. $8.00 – 10.00.

388 L.C., mark 31, dish 9½", wide gold lace edge on white $10.00 – 15.00.

ANCESTRAL, mark 54, plate 9", silver flowers and trim. Courtesy Sebring Historical Society. $9.00 – 12.00.

LUXOR, mark 20, sugar bowl with cover, silver design on Ivory Ware. $20.00 – 25.00.

LUXOR, mark 20, cup and saucer, silver design on Ivory Ware. $10.00 – 15.00.

NORMA*, mark 18, creamer, silver Art Deco design on white. $15.00.

PRISCILLA*, mark 1, plate 9", small gold flowers, seed pearl and scallop edge. $9.00 – 12.00.

GOLD ROSE*, mark 18, plate 6", small gold decal on rim, Puritan shape. $2.00.

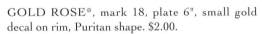

AMBASSADOR PERSIAN, mark 51, bowl 9½", narrow gold lace on red edge, 22K gold. May be other colors. $12.00 – 15.00.

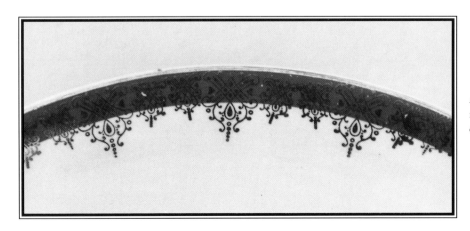

AMBASSADOR PERSIAN, full view.

AMERICAN AMBASSADOR GREEN, mark 51, saucer 6", narrow gold lace on green edge. May be other colors. $3.00 – 5.00.

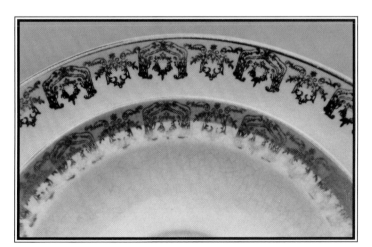

AMERICAN AMBASSADOR YELLOW, mark 51, platter 13½", narrow gold lace on yellow edge. Pattern close-up. May be other colors. $20.00 – 25.00.

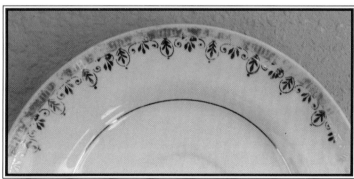

BUCKINGHAM, mark 31, saucer 6", narrow gold lace on pink edge. May be other colors. $3.00 – 5.00.

SOCIALITE*, mark 17 sugar bowl with cover, blue and gold trim, stamp 12 23. $25.00.

SOCIALITE*, mark 18, dish with cover, gold letter "D" on white, narrow blue and gold trim. $45.00 – 50.00.

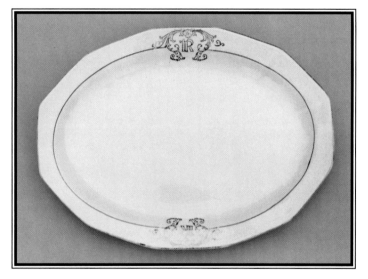

SOCIALITE*, mark 18, platter 11¾", gold letter "R" on white, blue and gold trim. Other monograms. $15.00 – 20.00.

SOCIALITE*, mark 18, sugar bowl, gold letter "E" on white with blue and gold trim. Other letters. $25.00.

GEORGETTE*, mark 18, sugar bowl with cover, small blue and green flowers, red line, and gold trim, stamp 5 22. $25.00.

COLLEEN*, mark 18, creamer, green flowers with orange ribbon, gold trim, stamp 3210. $15.00.

ARIA*, mark 18, sugar bowl with cover, assorted floral decals on sides and cover, stamp 12 27. $25.00.

HEIRLOOM*, mark 18, plate 9", framed flower basket, red line trim. $9.00 – 12.00.

FLORENCE*, mark 18, dish with cover, blue urn with flowers, gold line trim. $45.00 – 50.00.

FLORENCE*, mark 18, plate 8", blue urn with flowers, gold line trim. $9.00 – 12.00.

FLORENCE*, no mark, cup and saucer 6", blue urn with flowers. $10.00 – 15.00.

AURELIA*, mark 18, creamer, floral decal with blue trim. (8002P13 in gold). $15.00.

ROSINNE*, mark 18, creamer, floral decal with three roses, gold trim, stamp *7* 029-802 P 13. $15.00.

MEDALLION*, mark 18, sugar bowl with cover, small pink roses on blue, blue trim, stamp 563 B28. $25.00.

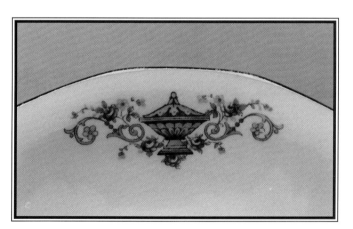

LISA*, mark 18, bowl 6", delicate floral decal, gold trim on edge. $5.00.

ART DECO*, mark 18, plate *7*", abstract design, blue line, and gold trim. $5.00 – *7*.00.

FORGET-ME-NOT*, mark 20, plate 9", urn filled with blue flowers, blue line, and gold trim. $10.00 – 15.00.

FORGET-ME-NOT*, mark 17, creamer, urn filled with blue flowers, 7-1928. $15.00.

PAULA*, no mark, bowl 6", floral decal in pink and blue, blue trim. $5.00 – 8.00.

PETUNIA*, mark 18, bowl 9", pink and blue petunias in blue urn, trimmed with two blue lines. $5.00 – 8.00.

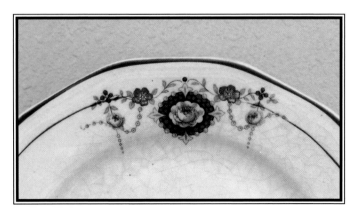

CORRINE*, mark 18, bowl 6", small pink rose decal on rim with two blue lines. $5.00 – 8.00.

SUSAN*, mark 18, plate 7", floral decal, blue line, and gold trim. $5.00.

SUSAN*, no mark, cup and saucer, floral decal, blue line, and gold trim. $10.00 – 15.00.

CENTERPIECE*, mark 18, plate 6", epergne with pink roses, gray line, and gold trim. $5.00 – 7.00.

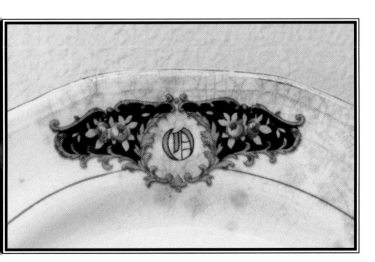

DUET*, mark 18, plate 7", letter "D" in cameo with small floral decal, red line, and gold trim. Made with other letters. $5.00 – 7.00.

DUET*, mark 17, sugar (no cover), letter "S" in the cameo with small floral decal, red line, and gold trim, stamp 8 23. Price quoted for both pieces in good condition. $25.00 w/cover.

TWIN ROSES*, mark 18, butter dish 8" with cover, small floral decal with two pink roses, gold trim. $35.00.

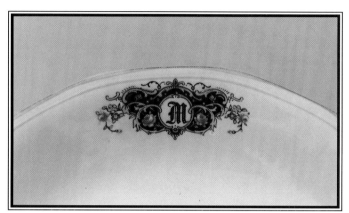

MICHELLE*, mark 18, bowl 9", letter "M" in the cameo with small floral decal, double gold lines, other letters. $5.00 – 8.00.

FOREVER*, mark 3, platter 10½", blue forget-me-nots on scalloped edge. $30.00 – 35.00.

BLUE & GOLD*, mark 20, serving dish with cover, gold daisies on blue trim, Ivory Ware. $35.00.

APRIL*, mark 17, gravy 8½", spring flowers in yellow and gray on sides, gold trim, with 18K gold. $15.00.

APRIL GOLD*, mark 18, gravy 8½", same pattern as April with gold etched trim, 8-27, 18K gold. $15.00.

SUMMERTIME*, mark 18, plate 7", three decals of yellow daisies on rim, gold trim. Courtesy Henry De Muth. $5.00 – 7.00.

SUMMERTIME*, mark 18, creamer, small yellow daisies, gold trim. $12.00.

SUMMERTIME*, mark 18, dish with cover, small yellow daisies, gold trim. $45.00 – 50.00.

ALAHAMBRA, mark 20, creamer, floral decal on yellow glaze with orange trim. Watkins collection. $12.00.

FLORAL 770*, mark 18, plate 8½", red, yellow, and gray on white. $9.00 – 12.00.

FLORAL 770*, mark 37, plate 6", red, yellow, and gray on Golden Glow. $5.00 – 7.00.

FLORAL 770*, mark 17, creamer, red, yellow, and gray on Golden Glow 1893 — B1GG. $12.00.

UNK 1962*, no mark, bowl 5½", multicolor flowers on Triumph shape. $5.00.

NASTRIUMS*, mark 17, plate 9", yellow ripple with flowers on trim. Ripple edge was patented by F.S. Sebring on July 8, 1927, under No 76,557. $10.00 – 12.00.

FLORAL 1260*, mark 17, plate 9" floral decal on rim, yellow glazing, dark blue trim. Watkins collection. $10.00 – 12.00.

MORNING GLORIES*, mark 17, plate 9½", floral decal, blue line trim on Golden Glow, made in 1928. $9.00 – 12.00.

MORNING GLORIES*, mark 17, creamer, floral decal on Golden Glow with a blue trim. $12.00.

MORNING GLORIES*, mark 17, plate 9", floral decal on Golden Glow Ripple Edge. $10.00 – 12.00.

MORNING GLORIES*, mark 17, creamer, floral decal on white with gold trim. $12.00.

MORNING GLORIES*, mark 17, butter dish 8½" with square cover, floral decal on white with gold trim. $35.00.

MORNING GLORIES*, mark 17, dish with cover, floral decal with gold trim. $45.00 – 50.00.

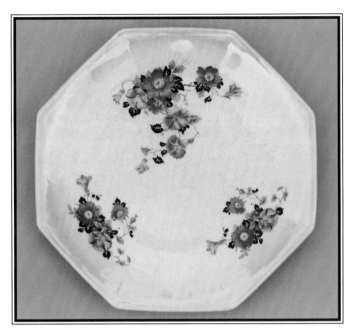

MORNING GLORIES*, mark 17, plate 9½", floral decal on luster with gold trim. On back "Compliments of Globe Furniture Co. Douglas, Ariz." $10.00 – 15.00.

FLORAL 1079*, mark 17, gravy, floral decal on Golden Glow. $12.00.

FLORAL 1079*, mark 3, pancake server 10" with cover, floral decal on Golden Glow. Eleanor Yaggi collection. $55.00 – 65.00.

SWEET PEAS*, mark 17, bowl 5", yellow and orange flowers on white, silver trim on raised edge. $5.00 – 7.00.

SWEET PEAS*, mark 17, sugar and creamer, yellow and orange flowers on white, silver trim on raised edge, stamp 4-32. $25.00 set.

EMERALD GLOW*, mark 17, plate 7¾", sweet peas on green glazing. $18.00 – 20.00.

EMERALD GLOW*, mark 17, cup and saucer 6", sweet peas on green glazing. $25.00.

EMERALD GLOW*, mark 17, milk pitcher 6¼" high, sweet peas on green glazing. $25.00 – 35.00.

CALIFORNIA*, mark 18, plate 6", red, yellow, and purple flowers on white with gold trim. $5.00 – 7.00.

CALIFORNIA*, no mark, pancake server 10" with cover, bright floral decal on Golden Glow. $55.00 – 65.00.

CALIFORNIA*, mark 17, serving dish with cover, bright floral decal on Golden Glow. $45.00 – 50.00.

CALIFORNIA*, mark 17, mug 4" tall, floral decal on Golden Glow, barrel shaped. $15.00.

CALIFORNIA*, mark 17, cup and saucer, bright floral decal on white with gold trim. $18.00 – 20.00.

CALIFORNIA*, mark 18, bowl 8", bright floral decal on white. $18.00 – 20.00.

CALIFORNIA*, no mark, platter 13½", bright floral decal on pink, Square shape. $20.00 – 25.00.

OLYMPIA*, mark 17, dish with cover, floral decal on Golden Glow, green trim. $45.00 – 50.00.

OLYMPIA*, mark 17, gravy, floral decal on white, trimmed with small blue line. $15.00.

PETIT FLEUR PINK*, no mark, platter 11½", small floral decal on Golden Glow, green feather trim on ripple edge. $35.00.

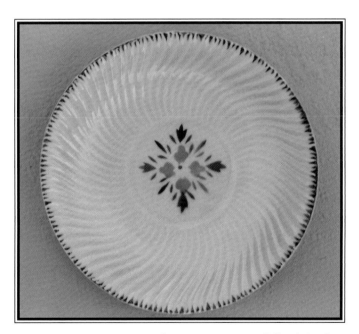

PETIT FLEUR PINK*, mark 22, saucer 6", small floral decal on Golden Glow, green feather trim on ripple edge. $5.00.

PETIT FLEUR PINK*, mark 22, pie plate 8½", small floral center. Three different patents applied for with this decor. The Golden Glow glazing, filed Nov. 7, 1927, by Harry J McMaster, Pat. No. 1,890,297. The feathered edge trim filed Nov. 26, 1930, by Charles O. Smith of Sebring, Ohio, Pat. No. 1,813,551. Ripple edge design filed July 8, 1927, by F.A. Sebring, Pat. No. 76,557. $25.00 – 30.00.

PETIT FLEUR BLUE*, mark 82, plate 6¼", small floral decal in center, blue feather trim on white. $5.00 – 7.00.

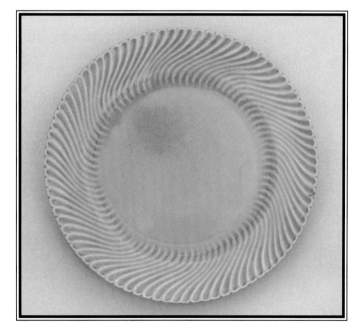

GREEN RIPPLE*, mark 17, plate 9", swirls in green glazing. Patent No. 76,557 filed by Frank A. Sebring for the Limoges China Co., July 8, 1927. Similar design also made in yellow. $18.00 – 22.00.

GREEN RIPPLE*, mark 17, milk pitcher 6½" and mug, solid color. $35.00 pair.

ROYAL MAZARINE, mark 13, teapot, cobalt blue with all-over small gold flowers. $75.00 – 85.00.

ROYAL MAZARINE, mark 13, sugar and creamer set, small gold flowers on cobalt blue. $55.00 – 60.00.

ROYAL MAZARINE, mark 13, cup and saucer 6". $35.00.

ROYAL MAZARINE, mark 13, plate 8", small gold flowers on cobalt blue. Set made for special order. $25.00 – 30.00.

ROYAL MAZARINE, mark 13, bowl 9", small gold flowers all over on cobalt blue. $45.00 – 50.00.

BLUE WILLOW, mark 18, plate 9", blue decal in center, gold swags on flow blue rim, Colonial shape, 1938. $25.00 – 30.00.

BLUE WILLOW, mark 62, plate, large decal in center, blue feather edge. $20.00 – 25.00.

BLUE WILLOW, no mark, cup and saucer 6", decal in center, blue feather edge. $12.00 – 15.00.

BLUE WILLOW, mark 62, platter 11½", blue design in center, gold swags on flow blue edge. $60.00.

BLUE WILLOW, mark 62, plate 9½", large decal on center and rim. $18.00 – 20.00.

OLD VIRGINIA RUST, mark 34, plate 9", large landmark, dark trim on light blue. Good Housekeeping Seal. Courtesy Sebring Historical Society, Sebring Ohio. $18.00 – 20.00.

OLD VIRGINIA RUST, mark 32, platter 11¾", landmark in rust on pastel green with dark trim. Courtesy Sebring Historical Society, Sebring, Ohio. $25.00 – 30.00.

OLD VIRGINIA MAROON, mark 33, plate 7½", landmark decal in maroon, dark trim on light green. Courtesy Sebring Historical Society, Sebring, Ohio. $15.00 – 20.00.

OLD VIRGINIA BLUE, mark 34, platter 11½", landmark in blue, dark trim. $25.00 – 30.00.

JIFFY POPPY*, mark 44, butter dish 7" x 3½", red poppies on white. $50.00.

JIFFY POPPY*, mark 44, set of refrigerator jugs 4½" and 6½", red poppies on white. Small one used for syrup and larger one for juice. $95.00 set.

JIFFY WARE, mark 44, jug 4½", assorted colors on white. Viktor Schreckengost design. $35.00.

C.D. POPPY, mark 61, plate 11", red poppies and red trim, stamp 1T359. $20.00.

MONTEREY*, mark 44, custard cup 2¾, red poppy decal on Jiffy shape. $8.00 – 12.00.

MONTEREY*, mark 44, waffle server 11", red poppies on white Jiffy Ware. $45.00.

LILAC TIME, mark 30, pitcher 6½" tall, pink and lilac floral decal on black ribbon, silver trim. $25.00 – 30.00.

LILAC TIME, mark 30, serving dish with cover, pink and lilac floral decal on black ribbon, silver trim. $50.00 – 55.00.

FRANCINE*, mark 28, plate 9¼", small flowers on purple ribbon, silver trim on pink glazing. $10.00 – 15.00.

PRIMROSE ORANGE, mark 30, plate 6¼", ring of small flowers on edge. 9Z133. $5.00 – 7.00.

CARNATION, marks 17 & 20, plate 10", large flowers on Ivory Ware with silver trim, stamp 3 30 and 1Z188. $10.00 – 15.00.

CLOVER BLOSSOMS, mark 35, platter 10½", pale flowers on pink with silver trim. $15.00 – 20.00.

APPLE BLOSSOM*, no mark, cup 3½", pink flower on pink Peach Blow, silver trim. $9.00 – 12.00.

ROSE MARIE, mark 27, plate 9", pale roses on pink, silver trim. $17.00 – 20.00.

MAY FLOWER, mark 30, cup and saucer 4¾", pastel iris on pink with silver trim, stamp 3M 133. Courtesy Marilyn Slabaugh. $15.00.

THE PANSEY, mark 27, plate 8½", colorful blue and pink pansies on pink with silver trim. $9.00 – 12.00.

ROSE MARIE, mark 36, gravy 8½", rose on pink, silver trim. $15.00.

SILVER MOON, mark 49, platter 15¼", pale roses on rim, pink with silver trim, stamp 3D 133. $35.00 – 40.00.

DAHLIA, mark 30, bowl 9½", bright flowers on pink with silver trim. $25.00.

PRIMROSE*, mark 37, plate 9" sq., bright flowers on pink with silver trim. $10.00 – 15.00.

GOLDENROD, mark 30, platter 11¼", yellow and green tall grass decal on pink with silver trim, stamped 1M133. $25.00.

CAROLINA ROSES, mark 37, platter 11", colorful flowers on rim, pink with silver trim. $25.00.

CAROLINA ROSES, mark 37, plate 3" sq., colorful floral decal on pink with silver trim. $15.00.

SILVER MOON, mark 29, plate 10" sq., pastel flowers on pink with silver trim, 1948 Trademark Reg. Ser #283497. $10.00 – 15.00.

SILVER MOON, mark 30, dish with cover, pastel flowers on pink with silver trim. $50.00 – 55.00.

DECEMBER SILVER MOON, no mark, sugar 4¾", similar to Silver Moon, on Candlelight shape. $15.00.

DECEMBER SILVER MOON, mark 28, sugar, pastel flowers on pink with silver trim, similar to Silver Moon. $18.00 – 20.00.

SILVER MOON, mark 30, ashtray 5", pastel flowers on pink, silver trim, stamp 4Z133. $15.00.

SYLVIA, mark 43, plate 10", pastel flowers on pink, silver trim on Triumph shape. Sandra Wuchnic collection. $10.00 – 15.00.

IDEAL, mark 26, cup and saucer 6" sq., bright flowers in black vase on pink, silver trim. $15.00.

IDEAL, mark 30, creamer and sugar bowl, bright flowers in black vase on pink with silver trim, stamp 1M133. $25.00 set.

IDEAL, mark 49, platter 11¼", bright flowers in black vase, fluted rim, silver trim. $25.00.

IDEAL, mark 20, saucer 6", bright flowers in black vase on white with trellis raised rim, stamp M25. $5.00.

BEL CLARE, mark 27, platter 8½", pastel flowers on pink with silver trim. $15.00.

BEL CLARE, mark 27, coffee server 8" tall, pastel flowers on pink with silver trim. Courtesy Terry Anderson. $50.00 – 55.00.

WINONA, mark 30, platter 8½", pastel flowers on pink with silver trim. $15.00.

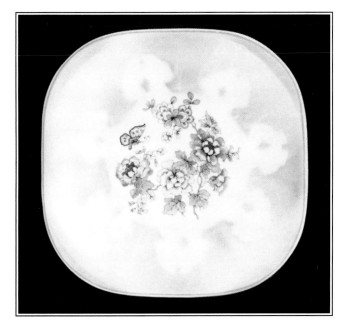

VIRGINIA*, mark 3, plate 6" sq., pastel flowers on white, pink and gray luster. Watkins collection. $9.00 – 12.00.

GLORIA*, mark 17, gravy 8¾", orange and gray floral, gold trim, stamp 2 31. $15.00.

CHARMAINE, mark 34, plate 8", swags of small pink roses, gold trim. $9.00 – 12.00.

CAMPSIS*, mark 17, plate 6", trumpet vine in orange and gray, gold rim. $5.00 – 7.00.

MONTICELLO, mark 20, plate 7", ring of colorful flowers, silver trim, stamp 8L 133. $5.00 – 7.00.

JOAN OF ARC, mark 49, gold fleur-de-lis with blue trim, made in 1934. Company advertisement photo. Unknown price.

BETSY ROSS, mark 49, plate 10", tiny red flowers all over, made 1934, silver trim. $9.00 – 12.00.

WILD STRAWBERRIES*, mark 20, teapot, delicate flowers and fruits decal with silver trim. Watkins collection. $35.00 – 45.00.

BLOSSOM TIME, mark 35, sugar bowl 5½", ring of pink flowers, silver trim on Ivory, stamp 9L133. Priced complete with cover. $15.00.

CHATEAU, mark 56, plate 9", pink roses with yellow circle, stamp 5G-NL, raised edge. Similar pattern as the Regency and 302-4M156. Courtesy Sebring Historical Society, Sebring, Ohio. $9.00 – 12.00.

302-4M156, mark 20, plate 9¼" sq., floral pink roses with yellow trellis, silver trim, on pearl ivory. Similar pattern as Chateau, the Regency, and Unk 1406*. $9.00 – 12.00.

THE REGENCY, mark 51, teapot, yellow trellis with circle of pink roses and wide gold trim. Similar pattern as Chateau and 302-4M156. $35.00 – 45.00.

UNK 1406*, mark 17, creamer, pink roses around yellow trellis, blue and gold trim. Similar pattern as Chateau and the Regency. $15.00.

BRIDAL WREATH, mark 72, plate 9½", ring of small pink roses around yellow trellis, gold feathered edge. Same pattern also stamped Vanity Fair. $9.00 – 12.00.

NEW PRINCESS, mark 31, platter 13½", small multi-floral decal with lines on rim, gold feathered trim, 1948. Similar to Golden Princess pattern. $25.00.

NEW PRINCESS, mark 34, pie plate 10", small multicolor floral decal and lines in center. $10.00 – 15.00.

NEW PRINCESS, mark 51, plate 6", small multicolor floral decal with amber lines on rim, stamp 4T 360. Similar to Golden Princess pattern. $5.00 – 7.00.

JENNIE LIND, mark 56, bowl 8", small pastel flowers all over, gold feathered edge. Courtesy Ed & Elsie Griffith. Pattern also spelled Jenny Lind. $9.00 – 12.00.

ENGLISH ROSE, mark 56, platter 15", small multicolor flowers in center and on rim, gold feather edge, 1948, stamp 7K GFE. $35.00 – 40.00.

CHINA POPPY, mark 56, platter 15", bright floral on white, stamp 3TCNL. Courtesy Helen M. Sullivan. $35.00 – 40.00.

UNK 1660*, mark 34, bowl 8½", ring of small roses, red and gold trim. $9.00 – 12.00.

UNK 1602*, mark 17, bowl 7½", ring of small flowers in green and pink on white. $9.00 – 12.00.

CHARM, mark 31, plate 6½", ring of multicolored flowers on maroon edge. Same pattern as The Charm 4090. $5.00 – 7.00.

THE CHARM 4090, mark 7, bowl 8", ring of multicolored flowers on maroon edge. Same as Charm, similar decor by other companies. $10.00 – 15.00.

DEBUTANTE, mark 51, saucer 6", ring of yellow flowers on white. $2.00.

SONG BIRD, mark 31, plate 9¼", small bird of paradise and flowers on rim, no trim. Pattern close-up. $9.00 – 12.00.

WHITE OAKS, mark 34, platter 11", small flowers and gray dots, light blue trim. $10.00 – 15.00.

WHITE OAKS, no mark, cup and saucer, same as previous photo, 1948. $9.00 – 12.00.

ROYAL OLD ENGLISH, mark 61, platter 13", small basket of flowers on beige rim. OLD ENGLISH is the same pattern on white. $20.00 – 25.00.

CROCUS, mark 19, plate 11", pastel spring flowers on rim, 1934. $9.00 – 12.00.

MELISSA*, mark 20, plate 7¼" sq., pink and blue flowers with gold trim on edge. $5.00 – 7.00.

MELISSA*, mark 19, plate 10", pink and blue flowers on rim, blue trim. $9.00 – 12.00.

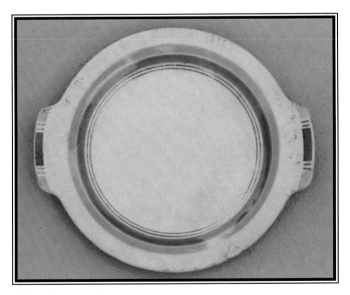

TITAN, mark 51, platter 11", gray, orange, and gold trim. $10.00 – 15.00.

SIROCCO, mark 56, plate 7¼", red and green feathered edge. Made in other colors. $5.00 – 7.00.

SIROCCO, mark 56, platter 12", gray and red feathered edge on white. Made in other colors. $10.00 – 15.00.

COMET, mark 51, silver stars and five red lines. Company Advertising Photo. Unknown price.

UNK 839*, mark 51, sugar bowl with cover, small geometrical design on yellow ribbon. $15.00.

SAILING SHIP*, mark 31, plate 10", hand-painted ship in center on Federal Coral Pink plate. Not signed, one of a kind. $40.00 – 45.00.

FEDERAL PINK, mark 31, platter 16", pink rim with gold trim, may be stamped Federal Coral Pink, found in other colors. 1940s. $25.00.

FEDERAL PINK, mark 31, coffee server, pink with gold trim. $35.00 – 40.00.

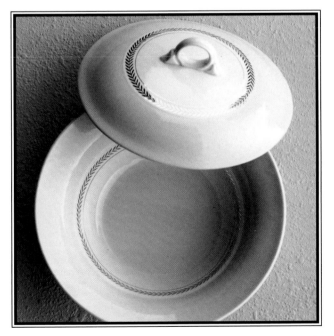

FEDERAL PINK, mark 31, serving bowl 9" with cover, pink with gold trim. $25.00 – 30.00

FEDERAL BLUE, mark 34, plate 10", blue rim with gold trim, 1940. Made in green, yellow, and pink rim. $9.00 – 12.00.

LYCEUM BLUE, mark 32, platter 13½", blue and gold rings on rim, 1949. Also made in rose, yellow, and green. $25.00.

LYCEUM ROSE-LC, mark 58, plate 9¼", pink and gold rings on rim, 1949. $9.00 – 12.00.

LYCEUM YELLOW, mark 32, sauce boat with attached dish 8¼", yellow and gold rings on rim, 1949. Also made in blue, rose, and green. $15.00 – 20.00.

DIPLOMA — ARABY BLUE, mark 32, plate 10", light blue rim with gold trim. Made in other colors. $9.00 – 12.00.

DIPLOMA — CORAL PINK, mark 32, serving bowl 10½" with cover, light pink with gold trim. Also made in other pastels. $35.00.

MELLOW GLOW, mark 61, plate 11", light blue rim. Made with other colors. $5.00 – 7.00.

TUSCANY BLUE, mark 61, saucer 6", wide rim with solid color. Courtesy Wilma Ellensburg. $5.00.

TUSCANY RED, mark 61, bowl 5½", wide red rim. $5.00.

TUSCANY YELLOW, mark 61, creamer, solid color outside, white inside on Triumph shape. Assorted colors within a set. $7.00 – 10.00.

TUSCANY GREEN, no mark, creamer, dark green outside with small gold lace trim, dripless spout on Triumph shape. $7.00 – 10.00.

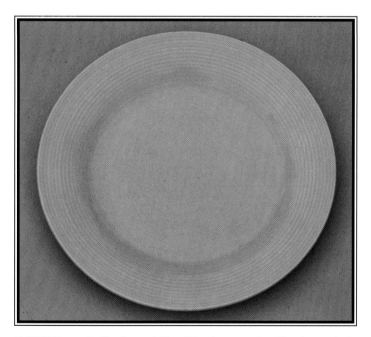

CAMEO, mark 48, platter 11", solid color, no trim. May be made in other colors. Similar to Fiesta Ware. 1939. $18.00 – 20.00.

MOOD — GREEN, mark 61, cup and saucer, rings of green shades. V. Watkins collection. $10.00.

MOOD — GRAY, no mark, salt and pepper shakers, gray trim on Triumph. $8.00 – 10.00.

ROYAL IMPERIAL, mark 32, plate 10", gold lace trim on beige rim. $9.00 – 12.00.

OSLO DUSTITONE BLUE, mark 34, plate 7½" sq., large pastel floral decal in center with light blue rim. Made with other colors. $9.00 – 12.00.

OSLO BLUE, mark 60, bowl 6", pastel floral decal in center with wide light blue rim, 1949. Made with yellow, green, and pink rims. $5.00 – 7.00.

NORWAY PINK, mark 60, plate 9½", large pastel floral decal in center with wide pink rim. Also made with yellow, blue, and green. Courtesy Sebring Historical Society. $9.00 – 12.00.

OSLO GREEN, mark 60, plate 6½", large pastel floral decal in center, wide green rim, 1949. Courtesy Debbie Hartley. Made with blue, pink, and yellow rims. $5.00 – 7.00.

OSLO YELLOW, mark 61, platter 13", large pastel floral decal in center with yellow rim, 1949. Made with blue, green, and pink rim. $20.00 – 25.00.

KAREN YORKTOWN, mark 61, platter 15½", gray abstract flowers, pink rim, 1940. Made with other pastel colors. $18.00 – 20.00.

FORD PINK, mark 61, bowl 7", pink and gray abstract flowers in vase, wide pink rim. Made with other colors. Courtesy Sebring Historical Society. $5.00 – 7.00.

COLONY T PINK, mark 61, sugar bowl with cover, ladies in colonial dress, pink trim. $15.00.

DELLA ROBBIA BEIGE, mark 34, gravy 8", fruit basket in beige and brown tones, wide beige trim. $15.00.

DELLA ROBBIA BEIGE, mark 32, platter 13½", fruit basket in beige and brown tones, wide beige rim. $25.00.

GRETA DUSTITONE BEIGE, mark 61, plate 7¼", abstract flower in center, wide beige rim. Made in other colors. Courtesy Sebring Historical Society. $5.00 – 7.00.

GRETA DUSTITONE ROSE, mark 61, creamer and sugar with cover, abstract flower with pink trim. Made in other colors. $25.00 set.

ETRUSCAN DUSTITONE BEIGE, mark 32, plate 9½", vase with flowers off center, wide beige rim. Made in other colors. $9.00 – 12.00.

ETRUSCAN DUSTITONE BLUE, mark 31, plate 9½", vase with flowers off center, wide blue rim. Courtesy Sebring Historical Society. $9.00 – 12.00.

MODERN CLASSIC GREEN, mark 51, platter 13¼", abstract gray cornucopia on green with green trim. Made in other colors. $25.00.

HARVEST MONSOON, mark 55, platter 8", abstract multicolored fruits in gray and red feather edge. Made in other colors. $10.00 – 15.00.

HARVEST, mark 51, plate 9¾", abstract multicolor fruits on yellow glazing, green trim. Similar pattern as Harvest Monsoon. $9.00 – 12.00.

PERIOD, mark 61, plate 9½", charcoal gray landscape on pink rim. May be other colors. $9.00 – 12.00.

TIGER LILY, mark 55, plate 10", large abstract flower on green decal, green feathered edge. $9.00 – 12.00.

JENNY LIND, mark 52, platter 13", abstract flowers with red and yellow trim. Name may be spelled differently. $25.00.

POND LILY MARINE BLEND, mark 61, platter 11½", lotus with yellow and light blue trim. Courtesy Nancy Pate. $20.00.

LAGUNA, no mark, plate 10", bright abstract flower center, fine gold trim, stamp G-1. Only name on backstamp. $9.00 – 12.00.

STARFLOWER, mark 61, plate 11", large pink and blue flowers off center, no trim. $9.00 – 12.00.

STARFLOWER, mark 67, platter 12" abstract flowers, silver trim. $20.00 – 25.00.

WILLIAM AND MARY, mark 61, bowl 8½", abstract flowers in pink, red, and gray, red and amber trim. $5.00 – 8.00.

INDIAN SUMMER, mark 61, bowl, 8", foilage and trim in red, yellow, and gray. $5.00 – 8.00.

INDIAN SUMMER, mark 61, cup and saucer 6", foliage and trim in red, yellow, and gray. $10.00.

JAMAICA, mark 56, teapot, abstract design in amber and green, no trim. $25.00 – 30.00.

JAMAICA SURF, mark 61, coffee server 9", abstract design in amber and green, wide yellow and green trim. $35.00 – 40.00.

RAVINE, mark 54, plate 10", orange foliage off center, no trim. *Good Housekeeping* Seal. $9.00 – 12.00.

RAVINE, mark 61, dish with cover, orange foliage and red trim. $35.00 – 45.00.

SAHARA, mark 19, plate 10", large floral decal in amber and gray off center. $9.00 – 12.00.

DAISY FIELD, mark 61, plate 11", yellow and orange daisies, red trim, stamp 1T359. $9.00 – 12.00.

BLACK-EYED SUSAN, mark 56, platter 11½", four yellow daisies on white, no trim, stamp 1K-NL, 1941. $15.00 – 20.00.

TOKEN PINK COTILLION, mark 34, plate 9", large pastel flowers in center, pink rim. Made in other colors on rim. $9.00 – 12.00.

FRAGRANCE, mark 34, plate 10", large pastel flowers in center, smaller ones on rim, no trim, made 1948. LC — no line. $9.00 – 12.00.

FRAGRANCE PINK COTILLION, mark 56, platter 12", large pastel flowers in center, wide pink rim. Courtesy Armande Meunier. $20.00 – 25.00.

FEDERAL SAMPLER WISHMAKER, mark 56, plate 9¼", petit point basket of flowers in center, smaller ones with serpentine border on rim. $5.00 – 7.00.

DEVON POINT, mark 61, plate 9½", large petit point floral decal in center, green trim, stamp 1T355. $5.00 – 7.00.

AUTUMN LEAF, mark 20, plate 6", made for Jewel Tea Co., similar to Hall China Co. decal. Unknown price.

DAPHNE, mark 34, serving dish 9", ring of large leaves around the edge. $10.00 – 15.00.

DAPHNE, mark 34, platter 13", ring of large pink leaves, gold trim. Also made in green. $20.00 – 25.00.

DAPHNE, no mark, cup and saucer 6", ring of large leaves on edge, gold trim. $5.00 – 8.00.

MAYFAIR WISHMAKER, mark 54, bowl 8", flower in center, red trim. $12.00 – 15.00.

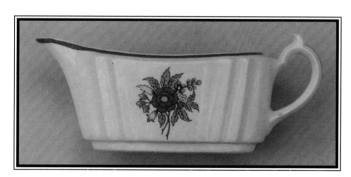

MAYFAIR WISHMAKER, mark 54, gravy, flower with red line trim. $8.00 – 10.00.

MONTE CARLO, mark 51, plate 9", red trim on white, used to serve snacks. $10.00 – 12.00.

FLOWER SHOP, mark 51, bridge set 9" with cup, small flower pots on steps, trimmed in red. Same pattern as Posey Shop. Viktor Schreckengost design. $20.00 – 25.00.

FLOWER SHOP, mark 51, bowl 5", flower pot with red trim. $8.00 – 10.00.

GOLD PALLADIUM, mark 79, saucer 6", Posey Shop pattern on Casino Shape, silver trim. The saucers are heart shaped while larger plates are diamond shaped. Made with other patterns. $3.00 – 5.00.

POSEY SHOP, mark 61, plate 7", small flower pots on steps, red trim, made in 1944. Same pattern called Flower Shop on Manhattan shape. Some pieces mark 60. $5.00 – 7.00.

POSEY SHOP, mark 61, soup plate 8½", small flower pots with red trim. $5.00 – 8.00

POSEY SHOP, no mark, cup and saucer, small flower pots on steps, Triumph shape. $8.00 – 10.00.

COTTAGE WINDOW, mark 56, platter 13½", bright flowers in squares. $20.00 – 25.00.

MARDI GRAS MONSOON, mark 56, plate 10", bright flowers in lattice, red and yellow feather edge. Made with other colors. $9.00 – 12.00.

A-9, mark 61, plate 11", bright flowers in center, wide 22K gold lace on blue rim. Similar pattern to Everglades. $10.00 – 15.00.

EVERGLADES YELLOW VISTA, mark 61, plate 6", bright flowers with wide yellow trim. Similar pattern to A-9. $5.00 – 7.00.

BERMUDA, mark 59, soup plate 8", yellow rim around bright flowers. $5.00 – 8.00.

BERMUDA, mark 59, platter 14", bright abstract flowers in center, yellow trim, 1943. $20.00 – 25.00.

BERMUDA, no mark, cup and saucer 6", yellow rim around bright flowers. $10.00 – 12.00.

BERMUDA, mark 61, gravy server, bright abstract flowers, wide yellow trim. (Note handles on bowl and under plate.) $15.00 – 18.00.

BERMUDA, no mark, egg cup 3", bright abstract floral decal, yellow trim. $10.00 – 12.00.

BERMUDA, mark 60, sugar bowl with cover. $10.00.

BAHAMA, mark 59, soup bowl, large abstract flowers, wide yellow rim. Similar pattern Regency Bouquet and Pompadour. $5.00 – 8.00.

REGENCY BOUQUET WISHMAKER, mark 56, platter 8½", large abstract flowers, amber trim, 1948. $10.00 – 12.00.

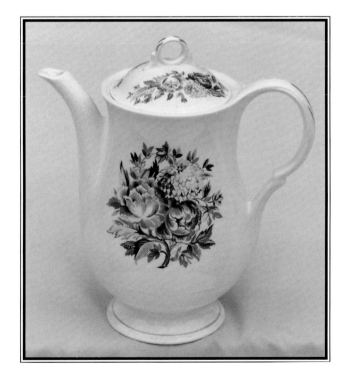

REGENCY BOUQUET, mark 46, coffee server 9", large abstract flowers, amber trim, 1948. Similar to Bahama and Pompadour Rose. $35.00 – 40.00.

REGENCY MONSOON, no mark, plate 10", large flowers in center, yellow and green feather edge. Similar to Bahama, Pompadour, and Regency Bouquet. $9.00 – 12.00.

POMPADOUR ROSE, mark 32, soup plate 10", large flowers, two-tone pink rings on edge. Courtesy Sebring historical Society. Similar to Regency and Bahama. $5.00 – 8.00.

POMPADOUR ROSE, no mark, creamer, flowers on side, pink ring at the base on Candlelight shape. Same as Regency and Bahama. $9.00 – 10.00.

COBURG DUSTITONE ROSE, mark 34, bowl 7", large floral decal in center, wide pink rim. Similar to Regis, Saxe, Wales, and Charlotte. $5.00.

SAXE COMMONWEALTH ROSE-LC, mark 34, bowl 7", floral decal in center, two-tone pink trim. Similar to Regis, Coburg, Wales, and Charlotte. $3.00 – 5.00.

REGIS YELLOW, mark 32, bowl 7", large floral decal in center, two-tone yellow rings on rim, made in 1940. Similar to Regis Rose and Regis Green. $3.00 – 5.00.

REGIS ROSE, mark 32, platter 13½", large floral decal in center, two-tone pink rings, 1940. Similar to Coburg, Saxe, Wales, and Charlotte. $20.00 – 25.00.

CHARLOTTE, mark 56, plate 10", floral decal in center, no trim. Similar to Coburg, Saxe, Wales, and Regis. $9.00 – 12.00.

CHARLOTTE, no mark, cup and saucer 6", floral decal, no trim. Similar to Coburg, Saxe, Wales, and Regis. $10.00.

CHARLOTTE, no mark, gravy 8", floral decal on sides, no trim. $12.00 – 15.00.

REGIS GREEN, mark 32, platter 16", large floral decal in center, two-tone green rings, made 1940. Similar to Coburg, Saxe, Wales, Charlotte, and Regis Rose. $20.00 – 25.00.

WALES, mark 56, platter 13½", floral decal in center, smaller ones on rim, 1943, stamp 7KNL A-50. Similar to Regis, Coburg, Saxe, and Charlotte. $20.00 – 25.00.

VICTORIA SURF, mark 61, coffee server 9", bright fruit compote, yellow and gray trim. $35.00 – 40.00.

VICTORIA SURF, mark 59, plate 8", bright fruit compote, yellow and gray trim. $5.00 – 7.00.

VICTORIA SURF, no mark, salt and pepper shakers 2½", decal on top, gray and yellow rings on the base. $12.00 set.

IMPERIAL VICTORIAN, mark 69, snack server 21½", colorful fruit compote decal in center, narrow white gold lace trim, framed with raspberries pattern on Farberware Aluminum, made in 1952. Assorted sizes. $35.00 – 45.00.

IMPERIAL VICTORIAN, mark 69, server 10½", colorful fruit decal in center, white gold lace trim, set in morning glory pattern on Farberware Aluminum, made in 1952, assorted sizes. $30.00 – 35.00.

IMPERIAL VICTORIAN, mark 69, bowl 10½", colorful fruit decal in center, fine white gold lace trim, in morning glory pattern by Farberware Aluminum. $28.00 – 30.00.

OLD DUTCH, mark 55, plate 6½", abstract red tulip in basket, red feather trim, stamp 5TC M.L.F.E. $5.00 – 7.00.

OLD DUTCH, no mark, gravy 8½", abstract red tulip in basket with red feather edge. $12.00 – 15.00.

OLD DUTCH, mark 81, basket 7", abstract red tulip plate set in Farberware Aluminum rose pattern. $18.00 – 20.00.

CONCORD, mark 64, platter 15½", large fruit basket in blue, no trim, Ann Orr design, 1943. $20.00 – 25.00.

CONCORD, mark 64, plate 9¼", large fruit basket in blue. $9.00 – 12.00.

CONCORD, no mark, cream and sugar, large fruit basket in blue, no trim, Ann Orr design. $25.00 set.

STRAWBERRIES, mark 38, platter 15¼", bright strawberry decal in center, cherry red band. $20.00 – 25.00.

ORCHARD, mark 32, platter 15", grapes with dusty green rim. Assorted fruits and colors. $20.00 – 25.00.

ORCHARD LIBAND DUSTITONE BLUE, mark 32, plate 7½" sq., large fruit decal in center, dusty blue trim, 1948, stamp LC-412. May be other colors on trim. $9.00 – 12.00.

ORCHARD, mark 73, plate 8", large fruit decal in center, light yellow edge. Watkins collection. $5.00 – 7.00.

NATIONAL BOUQUET, mark 59, covered dish, large decal showing 48 state flowers with yellow and green trim. $35.00 – 45.00.

NATIONAL BOUQUET, mark 60, plate 10", large decal showing 48 state flowers, yellow and green trim, made in the early 1940s. The starter set was advertised 20-pcs. for $4.99. $5.00 – 7.00.

ALTHEA, mark 61, plate 11", flowers in brown and yellow, brown trim, stamp 1T374. $9.00 – 12.00.

YELLOW DAISY, mark 56, platter 8", bright yellow daisies on rim, gold trim, warranted 22K gold. Pattern also made by the Sebring China on Golden Ware. $9.00 – 12.00.

YELLOW DAISY, mark 54, sugar bowl, bright yellow flowers on beige glazing, brushed gold trim, stamp 1 NG.W. $8.00 – 10.00.

BLUE DAISY, mark 67, plate 9½" large floral decal off center, gold trim, G-1 Warranted 22K gold. $5.00 – 7.00.

BLUE DAISY, no mark, cup and saucer, floral decal with gold feather trim. $10.00.

BLUE DAISY, mark 61, platter 13½", floral decal off center, no trim, 1948, stamp IT-NL. $18.00 – 20.00.

GREY BLOSSOMS, no mark, cup, large apple blossoms in blue and gray, gold feather edge trim. $5.00 – 8.00.

GREY BLOSSOMS, mark 55, plate 10", large apple blossoms in blue and gray in center, silver feather edge. $5.00 – 7.00.

LINCOLN CHINA, mark 39, plate 9½", pastel floral decal in center, gold trim. The Limoges China Co. used this name for special orders and exclusive decorations. $5.00 – 7.00.

INDIAN TREE, mark 56, plate 9", decal in center, gold sponge edge, K-G. W. 22K gold. $9.00 – 10.00

CHRISTMAS GIFT*, no mark, cup and saucer 4¾", green foliage with red berries. H & C gold stamp, was given as gift for the holidays. Courtesy Howard Baker. $10.00 – 12.00.

LYNNWOOD, mark 78, plate 10", large twigs in brown and gray. Hans Hacker design. $5.00 – 7.00.

LYNNWOOD, mark 78, covered dish, large twigs in brown and gray. Hans Hacker design. $35.00 – 40.00.

WOODLAND, mark 67, platter 12", large floral decal off center, no trim, stamp G-NL. $18.00 – 20.00.

CHOLLA CACTUS, mark 67, plate 9½", large floral decal in center, gold trim, stamp G-1, warranted 22K gold. $5.00 – 7.00.

IRIS, mark 19, plate 6¼", large flowers off center, no trim. $5.00 – 7.00.

PARAMOUNT, mark 61, platter 11", large pastel floral decal off center, green trim, stamp 1T 363. Courtesy Sebring Historical Society. $18.00 – 20.00.

THE CHATHAM, mark 61, plate 11", pastel flowers. Watkins collection. $9.00 – 12.00.

UNK 1386*, mark 61, plate 11", floral decal off center, green trim. $9.00 – 12.00.

SWEET VIOLETS, mark 67, plate 9¼", large bunch of violets off center, no trim, stamp 1-G-NL. $8.00 – 10.00.

BRIAR ROSE, mark 67, plate 9¼", large pink roses off center, no trim, stamp G-NL. Watkins collection. $8.00 – 10.00.

LORRAINE, mark 21, plate 10", large floral decal with two pink roses, fine gold trim. Similar to Marsh Rose pattern. $8.00 – 10.00.

LORRAINE, mark 56, plate 6¼", large floral decal with two pink roses in center, no trim. Similar to Marsh Rose pattern. $5.00 – 7.00.

MARSH ROSE COTILLION GRAY, mark 32, bowl 8", large floral decal with two pink roses in center, gold trim, wide gray rim, stamp TLC-414. Similar to Lorraine. $5.00 – 9.00.

LE FLEUR ROUGE, mark 55, plate 10", large single red rose with gold lace edge. Similar to a pattern by Hall China Co. $9.00 – 12.00.

AMERICAN ROSE, mark 57, plate 7½", single pink moss rose in center, forest green rim with wide gold lace. Similar pattern made by other china companies. $6.00 – 8.00.

VERMILION BUDS, no mark, salt and pepper shakers, small orange bud on top and gold rings at the base. $12.00 set.

141

VERMILION BUDS, mark 60, plate 9¼", four orange rosebuds with gold ribbon on rim, stamp 4TS324. Some pieces decorated with both Vermilion Buds and Vermilion Rose. $5.00 – 7.00.

VERMILION BUDS, no mark, cup and saucer 4¾", small orange rosebuds on gold ring. $10.00.

VERMILION ROSE, mark 59, creamer 3", orange rose and bud with amber and gray trim. $12.00.

VERMILION ROSE, mark 59, sugar with cover, orange rose and bud with amber and gray trim. $15.00.

VERMILION ROSE, no mark, cup and saucer, single rose with gold trim. $12.00.

VERMILION ROSE BELVEDERE, mark 61, bowl 8½", large orange rose with bud in center, gold trim. Give-away program, coupons from *The Buffalo Evening News* newspaper could be redeemed for china or matching glassware, 1939 – 1940. $6.00 – 8.00.

VERMILION ROSE, mark 61, plate 6", single orange rose in center, gold trim. $4.00 – 5.00.

VERMILION ROSE, mark 74, plate 6", single orange rose in center with gold rings on Victory shape. $6.00 – 8.00.

GOLDEN WHEAT, mark 59, plate 7", wheat and blue flowers, gold ribbon trim. Similar to Wheatfield pattern. $6.00 – 8.00.

WHEATFIELD, mark 59, platter 12", wheat and blue flowers, no trim. Similar to Golden Wheat pattern. $18.00 – 20.00.

WHEATFIELD, mark 55, platter 12", wheat and blue flowers, gold feather trim, 1948, stamp TC G.F.E. Similar to Golden Wheat. $20.00 – 22.00.

SUN VALLEY, mark 56, plate 10½", brown daisy and wheat in center with brown feather edge, stamp 1 K.O.G.F.E. Similar to Sundale and Kokomo. $3.00 – 5.00.

SUN VALLEY, no mark, cup and saucer, brown daisy and wheat in center with brown feather edge. $10.00.

SUNDALE TUDOR GOLD, mark 54, platter 11", brown daisy and wheat in center, wide gold lace edge. *Good Housekeeping* Seal. Similar to Sun Valley and Kokomo. $20.00 – 25.00.

SUNDALE TUDOR GOLD, mark 54, dish 9½" with cover, brown daisy and wheat with wide gold lace trim. *Good Housekeeping* Seal. Similar to Sun Valley. $35.00 – 40.00.

SUNDALE, mark 55, dish 9" with cover, brown daisy and wheat, gold feather edge, stamp 1K-G.F.E. Similar to Sun Valley. $30.00 – 35.00.

SUNDALE, mark 66, platter 8", brown daisy and wheat with wide lace trim, stamp 1-TC-S-264. $10.00 – 15.00.

SUNDALE, mark 54, plate 9", brown daisy and wheat center with gold feather edge. $8.00 – 10.00.

KOKOMO SUNDALE, mark 61, plate 10", brown daisy and wheat, ring of gold with wide yellow rim. Similar to Sundale and Sunvalley pattern. $8.00 – 10.00.

SUNDALE SURF, mark 61, plate 8¼", brown daisy and wheat center, brown and yellow trim. Courtesy Sebring Historical Society $5.00 – 7.00.

ELEANOR-T-GREEN, mark 59, plate 10", wreath of small flowers in center, gold trim, and light green rim, 1948. Similar to Filigree pattern. Made in other colors. $5.00 – 7.00.

ELEANOR-T-GREEN, no mark, cup and saucer, small multicolor flowers in center, gold trim, and light green rim. Triumph shape. $10.00.

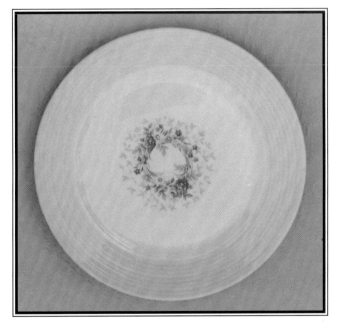

FILIGREE PINK VISTA, mark 59, plate 7¼", wreath of small flowers in center with pink trim. Similar to Eleanor-T-Green pattern. Courtesy Sebring Historical Society. $5.00 – 7.00.

JANIS, mark 55, bowl 6½", floral center with gold ring, pie crust edge. $5.00 – 8.00.

DOLLY VARDEN, mark 51, soup plate 7¾", tiny floral decals on rim, one in center. $5.00 – 8.00.

EMPRESS MIST COTILLION BLUE, mark 59, bowl 8½", tiny flowers in center, light blue side, stamp 1TS368W. $8.00 – 10.00.

THE ENGLISH ROSE 4060, mark 7, plate 6½", gold chain circle around small flowers, wide pink rim. $4.00 – 6.00.

BLUSH PINK, mark 32, saucer 6", small flowers in center, brown and green lines inside pink trim, 1943. Also marked Pink Blush. $3.00 – 4.00.

GOLDEN PRINCESS, mark 59, plate 9", small multicolored flower decal in center, double gold trim. Similar to Princess pattern. Courtesy Sebring Historical Society. $5.00 – 7.00.

TROUBADOUR, mark 32, plate 9", delicate flowers in center and on rim, wide pink rim, fine green and gold lines as trim, 1948. $9.00 – 12.00.

TROUBADOUR, no mark, gravy with attached plate. $18.00 – 20.00.

LYRIC BUDS COTILLION BLUE, mark 59, plate 9¼", small bunch of flowers with light blue trim, 1948, stamp B48 ST 1-2. $5.00 – 7.00.

LANGUGAGE OF FLOWERS, mark 21, plate 7", pink and blue flowers all over, pink trim. $5.00 – 7.00.

LANGUAGE OF FLOWERS, mark 32, platter 12", pink and blue flowers all over, pink edge. $15.00 – 20.00.

LANGUAGE OF FLOWERS, no mark, saucer 6", pink and blue flowers all over, black and gold lines on edge. $2.00.

LANGUAGE OF FLOWERS, no mark, covered dish, pink and blue flowers all over, black and gold lines on edge. $35.00 – 40.00.

LIMOGES PRIDE*, mark 2, vegetable dish, fine china, small pink roses with blue ribbon, gold trim. Made before the fire of 1903. $75.00 with cover.

NANCY ROSE, mark 32, plate 9½", small pink roses with blue ribbon, blue and gold trim, 1948. $3.00 – 5.00.

NANCY ROSE, mark 33, platter 12", small pink roses with blue ribbon, blue and gold trim. $15.00 – 20.00.

NANCY ROSE, no mark, cup and saucer 6", small pink roses with blue ribbon, blue and gold trim. $10.00.

NANCY ROSE, no mark, creamer and sugar bowl, small pink roses with blue ribbon, blue and gold trim. $25.00.

PURE GOLD, mark 56, plate 9", basket of flowers in center with gold edge, 22K gold. $9.00 – 12.00.

PURE GOLD, mark 56, teapot, basket of flowers in center with gold trim. $35.00.

GOLD CUP, mark 34, plate 8", basket of flowers with light blue and gold trim. $8.00 – 10.00.

WHITE GOLD, mark 39, plate 6¼", basket of flowers with silver ring of leaves, 1940. $4.00 – 5.00.

JULIET, no mark, bowl 5", basket of flowers on inside with gold lace trim. $10.00 – 12.00.

JULIET, mark 59, platter 12", basket of flowers in center, wide gold lace trim, stamp IT-S 350 – 30. Similar to UNK 1722* pattern. $25.00.

JULIET, mark 59, coffee server 9", basket of flowers with wide gold lace trim. $35.00 – 40.00.

TREASURE ISLAND, mark 61, cup, basket of flowers with pink and gold trim. On Triumph shape. Similar to Juliet pattern. $5.00.

UNK 1704*, mark 18, plate 6" sq., basket of flowers in center with turquoise and gold trim, stamp 10 25. $4.00 – 5.00.

ROYAL HOSPITALITY, mark 60, platter 12", pastel fruits and flowers in center. Watkins collection. $20.00 – 25.00.

BOUQUET BUDS, mark 56, platter 10½", pink roses all over, gold feather trim, stamp 7TC-GFE, 1948. $10.00 – 15.00.

BLACKBERRIES* FOREST GREEN, mark 57, platter 11",
flowers and berries in center, wide gold lace on dark green rim.
$10.00 – 15.00.

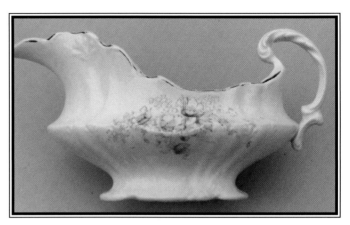

OLD LIMOGES*, mark 1, gravy, small flowers, gold trim.
$35.00.

KEEPSAKE, mark 56, plate 10", pink roses all over, gold feather
trim. Courtesy Howard Baker. $9.00 – 12.00.

BRAMBLE, mark 55, plate 6½", pink and blue roses on rim,
gold feather edge, stamp 3KGFE. 1948. $4.00 – 6.00.

CHINA ROSE, mark 56, plate 6¼", pink roses on rim, gold trim. $4.00 – 6.00.

BRAMBLE, mark 34, platter 12", pink and blue roses on rim, gold edge. $10.00 – 12.00.

WILD ROSE, mark 56, plate 6¼", pink roses on rim, gold edge. $4.00 – 6.00.

CATHY, mark 55, bowl 8", pink roses with baby's breath in center, gold trim, pie crust edge. Pattern also made by Hall China Co. Courtesy Sebring Historical Society. $8.00 – 10.00.

CHATEAU ROSE U G FOREST GREEN, mark 58, platter 14", large single white rose in center, wide gold lace on dark green rim, stamp 1T S350, warranted 22K gold. Similar to New Dawn and Silver Dawn pattern. $20.00 – 25.00.

SILVER DAWN, mark 67, plate 8", large single white rose in center, gold edge. Similar to Chateau Rose and New Dawn. $5.00 – 7.00.

NEW DAWN, no mark, cup, single white rose with dark green and gold lace trim. Similar to Silver Dawn and Chateau Rose. $5.00.

TRILLIUM FOREST GREEN, mark 57, platter 11", large single white flower in center, gold lace on dark green rim, stamp G-410. $18.00 – 20.00.

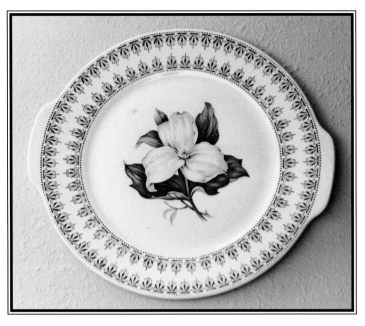

TRILLIUM, mark 63, platter 11", large single white flower, wide gold lace edge, stamp 1-T-S-530. $18.00 – 20.00.

TRILLIUM, no mark, cup, single flower, wide gold lace trim on Triumph shape. $5.00.

TRILLIUM, mark 67, plate 6½", large single white flower in center, gold trim on edge, stamp G-410. $5.00 – 7.00.

TRILLIUM, no mark, cup, large single white flower, gold trim on mandarin green, Corinthian shape. $5.00.

CANDLELIGHT, no mark, shakers 4½", light blue trim on white, matching several patterns, such as Tea Rose and Nancy Rose. $10.00 – 12.00.

OVINGTONS FIFTH AVE U G GRAY, mark 77, plate 10", large single white flower in center, wide silver lace on gray rim, stamp T-S351-135, GOLD PALLADIUM Warranted. $10.00 – 15.00.

DOGWOOD, mark 32, plate 11", white and green floral decal, gold trim, 1948. Also made on Triumph shape with light blue trim. $5.00 – 7.00.

DOGWOOD, no mark, creamer with cover, single flower with blue and gold trim. The cover was made for sugar bowl, also fits the creamer. $12.00.

GARDENIA, mark 32, plate 10", ring of flowers in white and green, gold trim, stamp 4LC-1. $5.00 – 7.00

GOLDEN TEA ROSE, mark 71, platter 11", large single rose in center, double gold rings. Similar to Tea Rose pattern. $15.00 – 20.00.

GOLDEN TEA ROSE, no mark, cup and saucer, single rose with gold trim. $12.00.

TEA ROSE PINK, mark 33, plate 9", large single rose in center, wide pink rim, 1949. $5.00 – 7.00.

TEA ROSE DUSTITONE BLUE, no mark, saucer 6", large single rose in center, wide pale blue rim, 1949. Made in other colors. Similar to Golden Tea Rose. $3.00 – 5.00.

TEA ROSE DUSTITONE YELLOW, no mark, bowl 5½", large single rose in center, wide yellow rim. Courtesy Sebring Historical Society. $3.00 – 5.00.

TEA ROSE DUSTITONE GREEN, no mark, creamer and sugar bowl with cover, single rose, light green, 1949. Made in other colors. $25.00.

RUST TULIP, mark 74, sugar bowl with cover, flowers with gold abstract design on Victory shape, same pieces made by Salem China. Piece shown is badly damaged, used for pattern sample only because it is very rare. $12.00.

161

SPRING TULIP, mark 19, bowl 9", spring flowers in bowl, red trim. $8.00 – 10.00.

TULIP TIME✳, no mark, plate 6¼", large pastel tulips in center, green trim on Triumph shape. Similar to Easter and Springtime. $5.00 – 7.00.

EASTER COTILLION PINK, mark 70, platter 11¾", large pastel tulips in center, wide pink rim. Made in other colors. Similar to Tulip Time✳ and Springtime. $10.00 – 15.00.

SPRINGTIME, mark 38, plate 6¼", large pastel tulips in center, wide gold lace trim. Similar to Easter and Tuplip Time✳. $5.00 – 7.00.

ARISTOCRAT, mark 67, plate 10", pink and red roses in center, gold trim, stamp G41l0 22K gold. Similar to Bouquet. $5.00 – 7.00.

THE ARISTOCRAT, mark 58, bowl 9", pink and red roses in center, wide gold lace edge, stamp 1TS530. $9.00 – 12.00.

ARISTOCRAT, no mark, cup, pink and red roses, dark green and gold trim. Candlelight shape. $5.00.

BOUQUET US BURGUNDY, mark 55, two-plate server, pink and red roses in center, dark red and gold trim. Similar to Aristocrat. $22.00 – 25.00.

EGERT ROSE, no mark, plate 10", large multicolored floral center, light green rim on Triumph shape, stamp 1T NL. $5.00 – 7.00.

SHARON, mark 54, plate 6¼", large flowers in center, no trim, made in white and beige glazing, stamp 1N-NL. $5.00 – 7.00.

LAMARR, mark 56, platter 13½", large multicolored floral center, no trim, 1949, stamp C-48. $12.00 – 15.00.

PRINCE RUPERT, mark 61, plate 8¼", roses in center, blue, beige, and gold lace trim. $5.00 – 7.00.

ARCADIA, mark 56, plate 7" large floral center with wide gold lace edge, stamp 1KS300 W 22K gold, 1948. Similar to Admiration. $5.00 – 7.00.

ARCADIA, mark 56, platter 11½", large floral center with wide gold lace edge, stamp 1KS300 W 22K gold, 1948. Similar to Admiration. $18.00 – 20.00.

ADMIRATION, mark 56, plate 10", large floral center, red and gold lace trim, stamp1-T S3364D-411 W 22K gold. Similar to Arcadia. $5.00 – 8.00

ROSALIE, mark 59, plate 6½", floral decal in center, wide gold lace trim, 1947. $5.00 – 7.00.

LAMARR, mark 55, plate 6¼", large multicolored floral center with gold lace edge, 1949. $5.00 – 7.00.

JUNE ROSE, mark 56, small plate 6½", flowers with gold feathered edge. $5.00 – 7.00.

JUNE ROSE, mark 49, platter 11", large multicolored floral center, gold lace edge. $20.00 – 25.00.

JUNE ROSE, mark 49, sugar bowl with cover, multicolored floral center, gold lace edge. $12.00.

WALDORF, mark 61, plate 7", floral center, wide gold lace trim edge, stamp R4441. Similar to Meissen Rose. $5.00 – 7.00.

MEISSEN ROSE, MAROON EMPEROR, mark 59, platter 12", bouquet flowers in center, dark red rim with wide gold lace trim. $20.00 – 25.00.

MEISSEN ROSE, MAROON EMPEROR, mark 59, plate 10". $10.00 – 15.00.

MEISSEN ROSE, MAROON EMPEROR, no mark, coffee server. $35.00 – 40.00.

MEISSEN ROSE, mark 59, serving bowl 9" with cover, bouquet flowers in center with blue rim and gold lace trim. $20.00 – 25.00.

SUNBURST, mark 61, bowl 8", orange roses in center, gold lace edge, stamp 1-T-S270. $5.00 – 8.00.

THISTLE*, no mark, cup, large flower, no trim, Glamour shape. Courtesy Howard Baker. $5.00.

TULIP CUP, no mark, cup, pink tulip on side, no trim. H. Baker collection. $5.00.

UNK 1772*, no mark, salt and pepper shakers 2½", small flowers on top, gold lace band on the base, Triumph shape. $12.00.

LYRIC, mark 56, plate 9½", small pink roses on blue decal in center with wide gold lace edge. Similar to Royal Lyric. $5.00 – 8.00.

LYRIC, no mark, cup, small pink roses on blue decal, gold feather edge. Similar to Royal Lyric. $5.00.

ROYAL LYRIC EMPEROR, mark 32, plate 10", small pink roses on blue decal in center, wide gold lace on beige rim, stamp 1LC-S-284-A48. Similar to Lyric. $12.00 – 15.00.

GOOD HOUSEKEEPING, mark 68, cream and sugar bowl with cover. $12.00.

GOOD HOUSEKEEPING, mark 68, plate 10", multicolored floral decal in center, gold lace edge, 1940, warranted 22K gold. Similar to Melody. Courtesy Linda Muldon. $9.00 – 12.00.

GOOD HOUSEKEEPING, no mark, salt and pepper shakers, white with floral decal on top, gold band on the base. $12.00.

MELODY, mark 70, plate 7", large multicolored floral center with gold lace trim, 1948. Similar to Good Housekeeping. $5.00 – 8.00.

IMPERIAL VIENNA ROYAL, mark 60, sugar bowl with cover 4", yellow and blue floral decal, beige and gold lace trim, warranted 22K gold. Similar to Vienna. $12.00.

LAMOUR, mark 60, platter 11", red floral wreath. $10.00 – 15.00.

LAMOUR, mark 60, dish with cover, red floral wreath. $35.00 – 45.00.

LAMOUR, no mark, shaker 2½", red floral top, gold trim base. $9.00 – 12.00 pair.

LAMOUR, mark 60, plate 9", red floral wreath, gold lace edge. $10.00 – 12.00.

FORTUNE, mark 34, platter 12", rosette of multicolored small flowers, wide gold rim. $18.00 – 20.00.

IMPERIAL FORTUNE, mark 34, plate 10", rosette of pink, blue, and yellow in center, beige rim with gold trim. Similar to Fortune. $10.00 – 15.00.

TOLEDO DELIGHT, mark 54, creamer, small pink roses on yellow decal in center, wide gold lace rim. Decal used by other companies. $10.00.

TOLEDO DELIGHT, mark 54, gravy, small pink roses around a yellow circle, wide gold lace trim. Same pattern found stamped Sebring China. $12.00.

TOLEDO DELIGHT, mark 54, vegetable dish 9", small pink roses on yellow decal in center, wide gold lace edge, 1941 – 1942. Similar to Delight, Royal Delight, and Commonwealth. $15.00 – 18.00.

TOLEDO DELIGHT, mark 54, plate 10", small pink roses around yellow design. $10.00 – 12.00.

DELIGHT, mark 32, soup bowl 8¼", small pink roses on yellow decal in center, gold lace edge. Courtesy Sebring Historical Society. Similar to Toledo Delight and Royal Delight. $5.00 – 8.00.

ROYAL DELIGHT, mark 32, plate 10", small pink roses on yellow decal in center with wide gold lace on beige rim, stamp C-47. Similar to Delight, Toledo Delight, and Commonwealth Blue. $10.00 – 15.00.

COMMONWEALTH BLUE, mark 34, plate 11", small pink roses on yellow decal in center, wide blue and gold trim. Similar to Delight, Toledo Delight, and Royal Delight. $10.00 – 15.00.

BUDDHA PREMIER, mark 61, plate 6½", orange floral center, gold trim on beige rim. Similar to Prince Charles and Commonwealth Red. $5.00 – 7.00.

COMMONWEALTH RED, mark 34, plate 11", orange floral center, wide pink and gold bands. Similar to Prince Charles and Buddha. $10.00 – 15.00.

PRINCE CHARLES, no mark, cereal bowl 6", orange floral center with beige and gold trim. $9.00 – 12.00.

PRINCE CHARLES, no mark, cup and saucer 4¾", orange floral decal with beige, orange, and gold trim. Russell collection. $10.00 – 15.00.

PRINCE CHARLES, mark 59, plate 10", orange floral decal with beige, orange, and gold trim, sold 1945 by Bullocks of New York. Russell collection. Similar to Buddha Premier and Commonwealth Red. $10.00 – 15.00.

UNK 1922*, no mark, plate 6", floral center with delicate gold trim. $5.00 – 7.00.

UNK 1922*, no mark, coffee server, floral decal with gold lace trim on Triumph shape. $35.00.

CHATEAU FRANCE, mark 55, platter 14", scenic decal in center, wide gold lace edge. $20.00 – 25.00.

CHATEAU FRANCE, mark 55, bowl 8", scenic decal in center, gold feathered edge, stamp 1 KGFE. $8.00 – 10.00.

CHATEAU FRANCE, mark 55, bowl 8" wide gold edge. $8.00 – 10.00.

CHATEAU FRANCE, mark 55, plate 7½" sq. $9.00 – 12.00.

CHATEAU FRANCE — MANDARIN GREEN, mark 55, plate 10", scenic decal, wide gold lace and narrow green edge. $10.00 – 15.00.

CHATEAU FRANCE FOREST GREEN, mark 55, plate 10", scenic decal in center, fine gold lace on wide dark green rim. $10.00 – 15.00.

CHATEAU FRANCE, no mark, cup, scenic decal, gold lace edge on maroon border, Triumph shape. $5.00.

SERENADE, no mark, creamer with dripless spout, romantic scene in center, narrow gold lace trim. Similar to China D'or. $12.00.

SERENADE, mark 50, plate 9¼", romantic scene in center, narrow gold lace trim. Similar to China D'or. $10.00 – 15.00.

CHINA D'OR, no mark, cup, romantic scene with gold lace on maroon trim, Triumph shape. $5.00.

CHINA D'OR, no mark, sugar bowl with cover, romantic scene with wide gold lace trim. Similar to Serenade. $15.00.

CHINA D'OR, mark 59, serving dish with cover 8¾", romantic scene with wide gold lace trim. Similar to Serenade. $30.00 – 35.00.

CHINA D'OR, mark 58, plate 7½" sq., romantic scene with wide gold lace edge, stamped IT-S 284. $9.00 – 12.00.

CHINA D'OR, mark 58, plate 10", romantic scene in center, wide gold lace edge, stamp, warranted 22K gold. $10.00 – 15.00.

CHINA D'OR, mark 58, cup and saucer 6", romantic scene with wide gold lace trim. Similar to Serenade. $15.00.

CHINA D'OR, mark 58, bowl 5½", romantic scene in center, wide gold lace trim on dark red border. $5.00 – 7.00.

CHANTILLY, mark 50, plate 6½", romantic scene in center, wide gold lace edge. $5.00 – 7.00.

CHANTILLY, mark 32, plate 10", romantic scene in center, green ring. $10.00 – 12.00.

IMPERIAL CHANTILLY, mark 69, snack server 18", romantic scene in center, white gold lace trim set in Farberware Aluminum, morning glory pattern. Made in 1952, assorted sizes. $35.00 – 40.00.

GARDEN WALL, mark 58, plate 10", romantic scene in center, wide gold lace on dark red rim, U G Burgundy stamp 1T-S 284CD. $10.00 – 15.00.

LOVE SEAT, mark 59, plate 10", romantic scene in center, wide gold lace rim. Decal made in Amsterdam, Holland, and signed Fragonard. Jean Honore Fragonard (1732 – 1806) was a famous French painter whose gallant scenes are still popular as decor for china. Both Love Seat and Garden Wall are copies of his paintings. $10.00 – 15.00.

FARM FAIR*, mark 17, plate and cup, child's set, animal decals, red flower trim on yellow glaze. Chickens are on the plate, playing cat and dog are on the mug. $40.00.

FARM FAIR*, mark 17, divided dish 8", playing bunnies, red flower trim on yellow glaze. Matching plate and cup. $35.00.

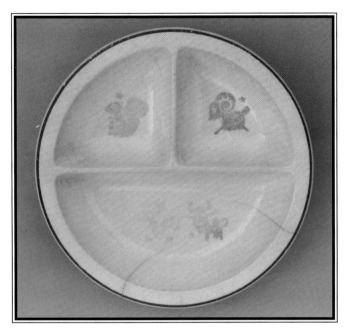

ANIMAL KINGDOM, mark 51, divided dish 8", Viktor Schrekengost design, animals and trim in red. Donkey, ram, cow, fish, squirrel, and elephant. 1940s. $35.00.

ANIMAL KINGDOM, mark 51, plate 8", cow and trim in red. $20.00.

LITTLE FRIENDS*, mark 18, plate 6¼", children on a bench, blue and gold trim. $18.00 – 20.00.

ICE CREAM, mark 3, plate, Neapolitan ice cream on napkin on green luster. Courtesy Saturday's Child Antiques. $175.00 set of six.

POND FISHES*, mark 3, plate 8¼", assorted fish decals with gold trim on flow blue. Made by other companies. Watkins collection. $35.00 – 40.00.

GREEN WATERS*, mark 3A, plate 8½", tropical fish decal, light green rim, gold edge. $20.00 – 25.00.

POULSBO*, mark 3C, bone dish 6¾", tropical fish with yellow and green trim. Courtesy Donna Driscoll. $20.00 – 25.00.

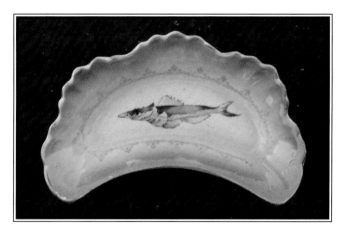

STURGEON*, mark 3C, bone dish 6¾", tropical fish decal with two-tone green trim. Courtesy Freighthouse Antiques. $20.00 – 25.00.

TURKEY*, mark 19, platter 13", large turkey decal in center, sometimes with gold trim or colored rim. $25.00 – 30.00.

UPLAND*, mark 3, plate 10", assorted game birds within a set, silver serpentine trim on edge. $20.00 – 25.00.

GAME, mark 18, plate 7", assorted game birds on luster by Daudin. A set may include 4 or 6 different designs, the golden pheasant is usually on the platter. $18.00 – 20.00 each.

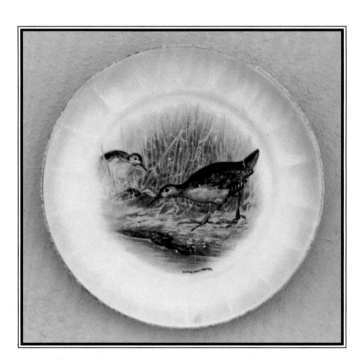

GAME, mark 18, plate 7", Virginia snipe? $18.00 – 20.00.

GAME, mark 18, plate 7", partridge. $18.00 – 20.00.

GAME, mark 18, plate 7", flying ducks on luster. $18.00 – 20.00.

CURRIER & IVES, mark 55, plate 10", winter scene, silver feather edge, gold palladium FE. $9.00 – 12.00.

CURRIER & IVES, mark 38, plate 10", winter scene, light pink rim. Made with other colors. $9.00 – 12.00.

CAPITOLS OF FREEDOM, mark 58, platter 14", cherry trees in Washington D.C., gold lace trim. Set made of different patterns. $30.00 – 35.00.

CAPITOLS OF FREEDOM, mark 58, plate 10", cherry trees in Washington, D.C., gold lace trim. $10.00 – 15.00.

CAPITOLS OF FREEDOM, mark 58, plate 6½", Eiffel Tower in the gardens of Paris, gold lace trim. $9.00 – 12.00.

CAPITOLS OF FREEDOM, no mark, saucer 6", Coloseum in Rome. $5.00.

CAPITOLS OF FREEDOM, no mark, cup, Casablanca decal inside cup, gold lace trim. $5.00.

CAPITOLS OF FREEDOM, no mark, creamer with dripless spout. $10.00 – 12.00.

CAPITOLS OF FREEDOM, no mark, sugar bowl with cover. $15.00.

DUTCH FARMERS*, mark 3, cider set, pitcher and mugs, assorted country scenes on white with blue trim. Watkins collection. $175.00.

BROTHER JOHN*, mark 1, pitcher 12", monk on brown tones. $175.00.

CHOCO CHERRIES*, mark 3, jar 6", cherries on brown tones. Watkins collection. $45.00 – 50.00.

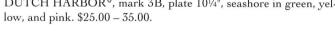

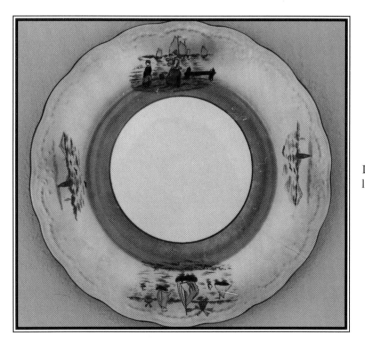

DUTCH HARBOR*, mark 3B, plate 10¼", seashore in green, yellow, and pink. $25.00 – 35.00.

OLD DUTCHWARE, mark 3B, pitcher 11", people on both sides, brown tones. "I Don't Like You Anymore." $50.00 – 60.00.

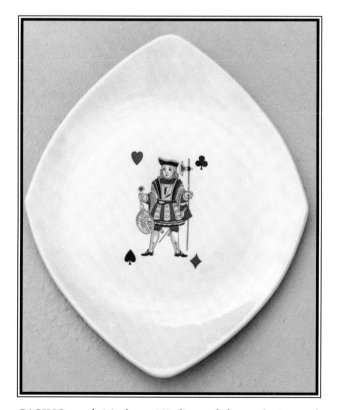

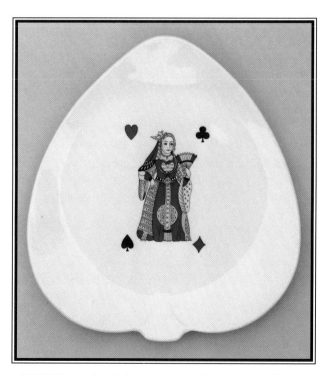

CASINO, mark 16, platter 12", diamond shape, playing card pattern, Jack. $35.00.

CASINO, mark 16, plate 10", spade shape, Queen. $25.00.

CASINO, mark 16, plate 10", spade shape, King. $25.00.

CASINO, mark 16, cup and saucer, cup has club shape, saucer 6" is heart shaped, no trim. $20.00.

CASINO, mark 23, creamer and sugar bowl with cover, small diamond shape, playing card pattern, no trim. $35.00.

SOLID GOLD*, mark 17, creamer, sugar bowl with cover, 22k gold all over. Watkins collection. $55.00 – 60.00.

MARKS

All backstamps are taken from wares, except where noted.

The backstamp or mark is the key to the identification of a piece. The American Limoges China Co., starting in the 1930s, gave complete data on each stamp: the company logo, the name of the shape, the name of the line and pattern, and sometimes the designer.

Until the early 1940s, stamping was done manually. It was a tedious job and when gold was used, it was expensive. Many pieces have no backstamp, within a set most small pieces, such as cups and saucers, have no marks.

At printing time, these stamps are known to be Limoges stamps. There are probably others. The dinnerware made for large companies (Sears and others) has their private stamp. The manufacturer cannot be positively identified without paperwork.

1. Ohio China Co., Sebring in E. Palestine, OH, mark still in use on 1909 calendar plate.

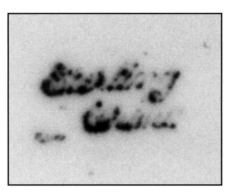

2. Sterling China Co., Sebring, OH, 1900 – 1902, used only on fine china.

2A. Sterling, 1900 – 1902

3. Limoges China stamp, green, used in 1903, found most often on dinnerware and souvenir items, 3A – Black, 3B – Blue, 3C – Red.

4. 1910, modern stamp.

5. Early mark, dates unknown, usually found on fine china.

6. 1902, re-used in the 1930s with U.S.A.

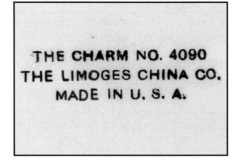

7. Date used unknown, stamp in gold letters.

8. 1902 – 1910, modern stamp.

9. 1910 – 1925.

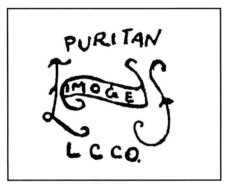

10. Used June 1917.

11. 1925 – 1935, quality stamp.

12. Used July 1925.

13. Used on special sets, cobalt blue.

14.

15. 1949 – 1955.

16. 1949 – 1955.

17. 1910 – 1930.

18. 1910 – 1930.

19.

20. 1930s.

21. 1949 – 1955.

22. 1930s.

23. 1949 – 1955.

24.

25. Used Dec 1, 1929.

26. On pink ware.

27. On pink ware.

28. On pink ware.

29. On pink ware.

30. On pink ware.

31.

32.

33. Good Housekeeping Seal, after 1941.

34.

35. Used 1928.

36. 1930s.

37. 1930s.

38.

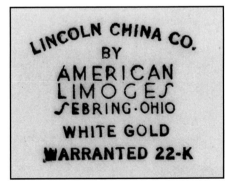

39. 1950s, name used for exclusive retail.

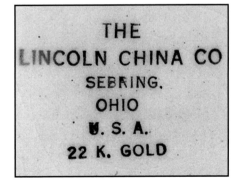

40. 1950s.

41. Stamp on dinnerware, 1945 – 1950.

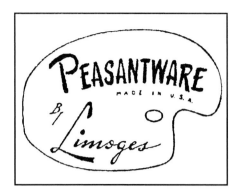

42. (Society for Historical Archeology.)

43. 1930 – 1945, found on Triumph shape.

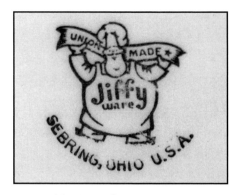

44. 1935 refrigerator ware.

45. 1936 – 1938 (Society for Historical Archeology).

46. Regency shape only.

47. 1946 – 1949 (Society for Historical Archeology, Vol. 16).

48. 1930s, used on Fiesta-like wares.

49. Shape designed in 1934 by Viktor Schreckengost.

50. Same mark used by the Sebring China Co.

51. Shape designed 1934.

52.

53. Used in 1943.

54. Used June 1941.

55.

56. 1942 – 1949.

57. 1936 – 1950, found on very ornate Triumph shape.

58. 1937 – 1950s.

59.

60.

61.

62. Underglaze.

63.

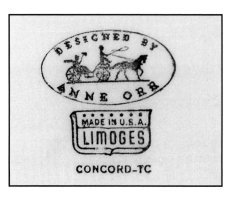

64. 1943, special design by Ann Orr.

65. Blue Willow stamp, in blue or brown.

66. Made for Eastern Columbia.

67. 1950s.

68. 1941.

69. 1952, made for Farberware Co., plates inserted in aluminum frame.

70. 1948, Melody pattern was made in that year.

71. 1949, Tea Rose pattern was made in that year.

72. Same decor as #75.

73. Exclusive retail mark.

74. Victory shape was designed for the Salem China Co. in 1934, very rarely used by the Limoges.

75. Same decor as #72.

76. Shape, introduced Jan 17, 1953.

77. Very ornate ware.

78. Hans Hacker exclusive design, 1950s.

79. Found on Casino shape ware with assorted designs.

80. Company name in gold letters.

81. Plate set in aluminum frame.

82. 1930s, similar to #22.

BIBLIOGRAPHY

American Ceramic Society. *The Bulletin.* Vol. 16, Jan. 1937, Number 1-23-H.B.B. File.

Anniversary Committee. A Brief History of the Town for the 50th Anniversary. Sebring, OH, c.1949.

Barber, Edwin. *Pottery and Porcelain of the United States.* NY: Putnamm's Sons, 1901.

Burgess, Irene. *Souvenir Plates, A Collector's Guide.* Private Publisher, 1978.

Butler, Joseph. *History of Youngstown and the Mahoning Valley.* American Historical Society, 1921.

Cameron, Elisabeth. *Encyclopedia of Pottery & Porcelain 1800 – 1960.* New York: Facts on File Publications, Cameron Books, 1960

Cunningham, Jo. *The Collector's Encyclopedia of American Dinnerware.* Paducah, KY: Collector Books, 1982.

Duke, Harvey. *Official Identification & Price Guide to "Pottery and Porcelain."* 7th Ed. NY: Ballantine Random House, 1989.

Gaston, Mary Frank. *Blue Willow,* 2nd Edition. Paducah, KY: Collector Books, 1990.

Kelly, Grace. "Limoges China Design by Schreckengost." *Alliance Review.* February 11, 1934.

Kovel, Ralph & Terry. *Kovel's Depression Glass & Dinnerware Price list.* New York: Crown Publishers, Inc., 1988.
___.*Dictionary of Marks Pottery and Porcelain.* New York, NY: Crown Publishers, Inc., 1953.
___.*Kovel's New Dictionary of Marks.* New York, New York: Crown Publishers Inc., 1986.

Lehner, Lois. *Complete Book of American Kitchen and Dinnerwares.* Lombard, IL: Wallace-Homestead, 1980
___.*Encyclopedia of US Marks on Porcelain, Pottery, and Clay.* Paducah, KY: Collector Books, 1988.
___.*Ohio Pottery and Glass Marks and Manufactures.* Wallace-Homestead, 1978.

Levin, Elaine. *The History of American Ceramics,* New York, NY: Harry N. Abrams Inc. Publishers, 1988.

Lund, Melvin. *Dinnerware Manufactures: Past and Present.* Ohio State University: Engineering Experiment Station News, Oct. 1946.

McCord, William. *History of Columbiana County, OH and Representative Citizens.* Chicago, IL: Biographical Publisher Co., 1905.

Mckee, Floyd. *The Second Oldest Profession, A Century of American Dinnerware Manufacture.* Salem, OH: Lyle Printing, 1966.

Miller, Robert. *F L E A Market Price Guide.* 5th Edition. Lombard, IL: Wallace-Homestead Books, 1984.

Miller, C.L. *THE JEWEL TEA CO.* Atglen, PA: Schiffer Publishing Ltd., 1994.

Newbound, Betty. *Gunshot Guide to Values of American Made China & Pottery.* Private Printing, 1983.

Opelia, Lynn. *"Happiness was Bluebird in 1900."* Collectors News, Nov. 1970.

Ramsey, John. *American Potters and Pottery.* New York: Tudor Publishing, 1947.

Rinker, Harry. *Warman's Americana & Collectibles,* 4th edition. Lombard, IL: Wallace & Homestead, 1990.

Gates, William Jr. and Dana E. Omerod. *Journal of the Society for Historical Archeology,* Vol 16, No 1 & 2, 1982. Courtesy of former president Harrison Keller.

Stiles, Helen. *Pottery in the United States.* New York, NY: E P Dutton & Co., 1941.

In the Potter's Field. Inhouse publication of the Chas M. Franzhiem Co., 1920.

"A Modern Story of the World's Most Ancient Art." Inhouse publication of the Limoges China Co., Sebring, OH, 1930s. Courtesy of former president Harrison Keller.

Whitmyer, Margaret & Kenn. *Collector's Encyclopedia of Hall China.* Paducah, KY: Collector Books, 1989.

Woodard, Dannie and Billie J. Wood. *Hammered Aluminum.* Wolfe City, TX: Henington Publishing Co., 1983.

ABOUT THE AUTHOR

Raymonde Limoges, born and educated in France, settled in Puyallup, Washington, over 30 years ago. A longtime dealer of fine china and familiar with the Limoges porcelain from France, her discovery of the American Limoges in 1982 began her fascination and quest to learn all she could about the china. Although Raymonde has retired as an antiques dealer and importer of fine china, she continues to collect American Limoges and now has more than 2,000 pieces in her collection. She is not only an historian and writer, she is also a board member and consultant for several museums and has been a Trustee for the Washington Trust for Historical Preservation.

In addition to her passion for fine china, Raymonde is past president of the Tacoma Opera Guild and has been a board member for many years. She and her husband, George, also an avid collector, are both fanatic gardeners. Their home has been declared a Certified Backyard Habitat from the National Wildlife Federation and a Wildlife Sanctuary by the Washington State Department of Fish and Wildlife; it is also home to many critters, a large collection of native plants, and rhododendrons.

INDEX OF PATTERNS

BOOKS ON COLLECTIBLES

This is only a partial listing of the books on antiques that are available from Collector Books. All books are well illustrated and contain current values. Most of the following books are available from your local bookseller, antique dealer, or public library. If you are unable to locate certain titles in your area, you may order by mail from COLLECTOR BOOKS, P.O. Box 3009, Paducah, KY 42002-3009. Customers with Visa or MasterCard may phone in orders from 7:00–4:00 CST, Monday–Friday, Toll Free 1-800-626-5420. Add $2.00 for postage for the first book ordered and $0.30 for each additional book. Include item number, title, and price when ordering. Allow 14 to 21 days for delivery.

DOLLS, FIGURES & TEDDY BEARS

2382	**Advertising Dolls**, Identification & Values, Robison & Sellers	$9.95
2079	**Barbie** Doll Fashions, Volume I, Eames	$24.95
3957	**Barbie** Exclusives, Rana	$18.95
3310	**Black Dolls**, 1820–1991, Perkins	$17.95
3873	**Black Dolls**, Book II, Perkins	$17.95
3810	**Chatty Cathy** Dolls, Lewis	$15.95
2021	Collector's **Male Action Figures**, Manos	$14.95
1529	Collector's Encyclopedia of **Barbie** Dolls, DeWein	$19.95
3727	Collector's Guide to **Ideal Dolls**, Izen	$18.95
3728	Collector's Guide to Miniature **Teddy Bears**, Powell	$17.95
4506	**Dolls in Uniform**, Bourgeois	$18.95
3967	Collector's Guide to **Trolls**, Peterson	$19.95
1067	**Madame Alexander** Dolls, Smith	$19.95
3971	**Madame Alexander** Dolls Price Guide #20, Smith	$9.95
2185	**Modern Collector's** Dolls I, Smith	$17.95
2186	**Modern Collector's** Dolls II, Smith	$17.95
2187	**Modern Collector's** Dolls III, Smith	$17.95
2188	**Modern Collector's** Dolls IV, Smith	$17.95
2189	**Modern Collector's** Dolls V, Smith	$17.95
3733	**Modern Collector's** Dolls, Sixth Series, Smith	$24.95
3991	**Modern Collector's** Dolls, Seventh Series, Smith	$24.95
3472	**Modern Collector's** Dolls Update, Smith	$9.95
3972	Patricia Smith's **Doll Values**, Antique to Modern, 11th Edition	$12.95
3826	Story of **Barbie**, Westenhouser	$19.95
1513	**Teddy Bears & Steiff** Animals, Mandel	$9.95
1817	**Teddy Bears & Steiff** Animals, 2nd Series, Mandel	$19.95
2084	**Teddy Bears, Annalee's & Steiff** Animals, 3rd Series, Mandel	$19.95
1808	Wonder of **Barbie**, Manos	$9.95
1430	World of **Barbie** Dolls, Manos	$9.95

TOYS, MARBLES & CHRISTMAS COLLECTIBLES

3427	**Advertising Character** Collectibles, Dotz	$17.95
2333	Antique & Collector's **Marbles**, 3rd Ed., Grist	$9.95
3827	Antique & Collector's **Toys**, 1870–1950, Longest	$24.95
3956	**Baby Boomer Games**, Identification & Value Guide, Polizzi	$24.95
1514	Character **Toys** & Collectibles, Longest	$19.95
1750	Character **Toys** & Collector's, 2nd Series, Longest	$19.95
3717	**Christmas** Collectibles, 2nd Edition, Whitmyer	$24.95
1752	**Christmas** Ornaments, Lights & Decorations, Johnson	$19.95
3874	Collectible Coca-Cola Toy **Trucks**, deCourtivron	$24.95
2338	Collector's Encyclopedia of **Disneyana**, Longest, Stern	$24.95
2151	Collector's Guide to **Tootsietoys**, Richter	$16.95
3436	Grist's Big Book of **Marbles**	$19.95
3970	Grist's Machine-Made & Contemporary **Marbles**, 2nd Ed.	$9.95
3732	**Matchbox®** Toys, 1948 to 1993, Johnson	$18.95
3823	**Mego** Toys, An Illustrated Value Guide, Chrouch	15.95
1540	**Modern Toys** 1930–1980, Baker	$19.95
3888	**Motorcycle** Toys, Antique & Contemporary, Gentry/Downs	$18.95
3891	Schroeder's Collectible **Toys**, Antique to Modern Price Guide	$17.95
1886	Stern's Guide to **Disney** Collectibles	$14.95
2139	Stern's Guide to **Disney** Collectibles, 2nd Series	$14.95
3975	Stern's Guide to **Disney** Collectibles, 3rd Series	$18.95
2028	**Toys**, Antique & Collectible, Longest	$14.95
3975	**Zany Characters** of the Ad World, Lamphier	$16.95

JEWELRY, HATPINS, WATCHES & PURSES

1712	Antique & Collector's **Thimbles** & Accessories, Mathis	$19.95
1748	Antique **Purses**, Revised Second Ed., Holiner	$19.95
1278	Art Nouveau & Art Deco **Jewelry**, Baker	$9.95
3875	Collecting Antique **Stickpins**, Kerins	$16.95
3722	Collector's Ency. of **Compacts, Carryalls & Face Powder Boxes**, Mueller	$24.95
3992	Complete Price Guide to **Watches**, #15, Shugart	$21.95
1716	Fifty Years of Collector's **Fashion Jewelry**, 1925-1975, Baker	$19.95
1424	**Hatpins** & Hatpin Holders, Baker	$9.95
1181	100 Years of Collectible **Jewelry**, Baker	$9.95
2348	20th Century Fashionable Plastic **Jewelry**, Baker	$19.95
3830	Vintage **Vanity Bags & Purses**, Gerson	$24.95

FURNITURE

1457	American **Oak** Furniture, McNerney	$9.95
3716	American **Oak** Furniture, Book II, McNerney	$12.95
1118	Antique **Oak** Furniture, Hill	$7.95
2132	Collector's Encyclopedia of **American** Furniture, Vol. I, Swedberg	$24.95
2271	Collector's Encyclopedia of **American** Furniture, Vol. II, Swedberg	$24.95
3720	Collector's Encyclopedia of **American** Furniture, Vol. III, Swedberg	$24.95
1437	Collector's Guide to **Country** Furniture, Raycraft	$9.95
3878	Collector's Guide to **Oak** Furniture, George	$12.95
1755	Furniture of the **Depression Era**, Swedberg	$19.95
3906	**Heywood-Wakefield** Modern Furniture, Rouland	$18.95
1965	**Pine** Furniture, Our American Heritage, McNerney	$14.95
1885	**Victorian** Furniture, Our American Heritage, McNerney	$9.95
3829	**Victorian** Furniture, Our American Heritage, Book II, McNerney	$9.95
3869	**Victorian** Furniture books, 2 volume set, McNerney	$19.90

INDIANS, GUNS, KNIVES, TOOLS, PRIMITIVES

1868	Antique **Tools,** Our American Heritage, McNerney	$9.95
2015	Archaic **Indian** Points & Knives, Edler	$14.95
1426	**Arrowheads** & Projectile Points, Hothem	$7.95
1668	**Flint Blades** & Projectile Points of the North American Indian, Tully	$24.95
2279	**Indian** Artifacts of the Midwest, Hothem	$14.95
3885	**Indian** Artifacts of the Midwest, Book II, Hothem	$16.95
1964	**Indian** Axes & Related Stone Artifacts, Hothem	$14.95
2023	**Keen Kutter** Collectibles, Heuring	$14.95
3887	**Modern Guns,** Identification & Values, 10th Ed., Quertermous	$12.95
2164	**Primitives,** Our American Heritage, McNerney	$9.95
1759	**Primitives,** Our American Heritage, Series II, McNerney	$14.95
3325	Standard **Knife** Collector's Guide, 2nd Ed., Ritchie & Stewart	$12.95 .

PAPER COLLECTIBLES & BOOKS

1441	Collector's Guide to **Post Cards**, Wood	$9.95
2081	Guide to Collecting **Cookbooks**, Allen	$14.95
3969	Huxford's **Old Book** Value Guide, 7th Ed.	$19.95
3821	Huxford's **Paperback** Value Guide	$19.95
2080	Price Guide to **Cookbooks & Recipe Leaflets**, Dickinson	$9.95
2346	**Sheet Music** Reference & Price Guide, Pafik & Guiheen	$18.95

OTHER COLLECTIBLES

2280	Advertising **Playing Cards**, Grist	$16.95
2269	Antique **Brass & Copper** Collectibles, Gaston	$16.95
1880	Antique **Iron**, McNerney	$9.95
3872	Antique **Tins**, Dodge	$24.95
1714	**Black** Collectibles, Gibbs	$19.95
1128	**Bottle** Pricing Guide, 3rd Ed., Cleveland	$7.95
3959	**Cereal Box** Bonanza, The 1950's, Bruce	$19.95
3718	Collector's **Aluminum**, Grist	$16.95
3445	Collectible **Cats**, An Identification & Value Guide, Fyke	$18.95
1634	Collector's Ency. of Figural & Novelty **Salt & Pepper Shakers**, Davern	$19.95
2020	Collector's Ency. of Figural & Novelty **Salt & Pepper Shakers**, Vol. II, Davern	$19.95
2018	Collector's Encyclopedia of **Granite Ware**, Greguire	$24.95
3430	Collector's Encyclopedia of **Granite Ware**, Book II, Greguire	$24.95
3879	Collector's Guide to Antique **Radios**, 3rd Ed., Bunis	$18.95
1916	Collector's Guide to **Art Deco**, Gaston	$14.95
3880	Collector's Guide to **Cigarette Lighters**, Flanagan	$17.95
1537	Collector's Guide to **Country Baskets**, Raycraft	$9.95
3966	Collector's Guide to **Inkwells**, Identification & Values, Badders	$18.95
3881	Collector's Guide to **Novelty Radios**, Bunis/Breed	$18.95
3729	Collector's Guide to **Snow Domes**, Guarnaccia	$18.95
3730	Collector's Guide to **Transistor Radios**, Bunis	$15.95
2276	**Decoys**, Kangas	$24.95
1629	**Doorstops**, Identification & Values, Bertoia	$9.95
3968	**Fishing Lure** Collectibles, Murphy/Edmisten	$24.95
3817	**Flea Market Trader**, 9th Ed., Huxford	$12.95
3819	**General Store** Collectibles, Wilson	$24.95
2215	Goldstein's **Coca-Cola** Collectibles	$16.95
3884	Huxford's Collector's **Advertising**, 2nd Ed.	$24.95
2216	**Kitchen Antiques**, 1790–1940, McNerney	$14.95
1782	1,000 **Fruit Jars**, 5th Edition, Schroeder	$5.95
3321	Ornamental & Figural **Nutcrackers**, Rittenhouse	$16.95
2026	**Railroad** Collectibles, 4th Ed., Baker	$14.95
1632	**Salt & Pepper Shakers**, Guarnaccia	$9.95
1888	**Salt & Pepper Shakers** II, Identification & Value Guide, Book II, Guarnaccia	$14.95
2220	**Salt & Pepper Shakers** III, Guarnaccia	$14.95
3443	**Salt & Pepper Shakers** IV, Guarnaccia	$18.95
2096	**Silverplated Flatware**, Revised 4th Edition, Hagan	$14.95
1922	Standard **Old Bottle** Price Guide, Sellari	$14.95
3892	**Toy & Miniature Sewing Machines**, Thomas	$18.95
3828	Value Guide to **Advertising Memorabilia**, Summers	$18.95
3977	Value Guide to **Gas Station** Memorabilia	$24.95
3444	**Wanted to Buy**, 5th Edition	$9.95

Schroeder's ANTIQUES Price Guide

... is the #1 best-selling antiques & collectibles value guide on the market today, and here's why . . .

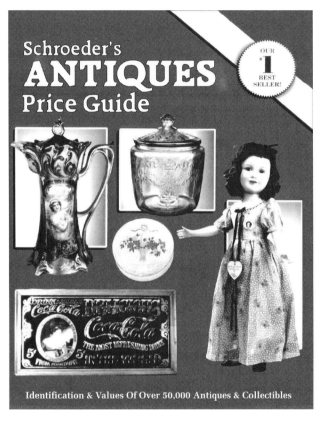

Schroeder's ANTIQUES Price Guide

OUR #1 BEST SELLER!

Identification & Values Of Over 50,000 Antiques & Collectibles

8½ x 11, 608 Pages, $14.95

- *More than 300 advisors, well-known dealers, and top-notch collectors work together with our editors to bring you accurate information regarding pricing and identification.*

- *More than 45,000 items in almost 500 categories are listed along with hundreds of sharp original photos that illustrate not only the rare and unusual, but the common, popular collectibles as well.*

- *Each large close-up shot shows important details clearly. Every subject is represented with histories and background information, a feature not found in any of our competitors' publications.*

- *Our editors keep abreast of newly developing trends, often adding several new categories a year as the need arises.*

If it merits the interest of today's collector, you'll find it in *Schroeder's*. And you can feel confident that the information we publish is up to date and accurate. Our advisors thoroughly check each category to spot inconsistencies, listings that may not be entirely reflective of market dealings, and lines too vague to be of merit. Only the best of the lot remains for publication.

Without doubt, you'll find
SCHROEDER'S ANTIQUES PRICE GUIDE
the only one to buy for
reliable information and values.

COLLECTOR BOOKS
A Division of Schroeder Publishing Co., Inc.